8 CRITICAL LIFETIME DECISIONS

*Choices
that will
affect the
quality of
your life*

RALPH PALMEN

Beacon Hill Press of Kansas City
Kansas City, Missouri

Copyright 2001
by Beacon Hill Press of Kansas City

ISBN 083-411-9315

Printed in the
United States of America

Cover Design: Paul Franitza

Library of Congress Cataloging-in-Publication Data

Palmen, Ralph.
    8 critical lifetime decisions : choices that will affect the quality of your life / Ralph Palmen.
        p. cm.
    ISBN 0-8341-1931-5 (pb.)
    1. Quality of life. 2. Decision making. I. Title: Eight critical lifetime decisions. II. Title.
    BF637.C5 P34 2001
    158.1—dc21

                                                    2001043871

10   9   8   7   6   5   4   3   2   1

CONTENTS

ABOUT THE AUTHOR

Ralph Palmen is a professional speaker who has been featured at more than 2,000 business meetings and conferences throughout North America and Europe. His videotape training programs include "The Art of Successful Recruiting," "Contract Employees," and "Interview Smart—Hire Right," which was nominated in 1992 by the American Library Assocation as "Best How-to Video of the Year." He has also authored *Principles and Success Strategies for Everyday Living.*

Palmen's success as a businessman includes his building a thriving chain of executive recruiting offices, and helping increase annual sales for a real estate company from $49 million to $242 million within three years. He was instrumental in organizing Express Personnel Service, which is now the largest independently owned staffing company in the United States. In 1979 he founded The Palmen Institute, dedicated to helping in the growth of individuals and companies. Palmen's business acumen has also been honored by *Time* magazine and the Seattle Chamber of Commerce as a Newsmaker of Tomorrow.

He has served his local church as Sunday School teacher, church board member, church treasurer, and a member of various committees. He is president of the Northwest Nazarene University Foundation Board.

Palmen and his wife, Darlys, live near Seattle. They have three children and three grandchildren.

To my parents, Earl and Ruth Palmen,
who taught me at an early age
the value of making good decisions
and wise choices,
and to my wife, Darlys,
who has been a wonderful sounding board
for the major decisions of my life
and a great model of the qualities of a great friend.

ACKNOWLEDGMENTS

A book is always the result of many people working together, so it is hard to single out a few people for special recognition when there are so many you should thank. Those whom I must especially recognize include Mark Cutshall, whose ability to edit and critique the early drafts of the manuscript were invaluable; my sister Jerilyn Tyner, whose helpful suggestions on writing technique were a great help; and Kathy Heywood, who, in addition to her typing and editing skills, gave me a great attitudinal boost with her encouragement. Her inspiration was just what I needed to finish the manuscript and get it ready for publication.

I would also like to thank several of the great team at Beacon Hill Press of Kansas City—Bonnie Perry, Judi Perry, Jonathan Wright, Jeanette Littleton, and Bruce Nuffer—for all their help.

And finally I wish to thank all the friends who have come alongside me down through the years. It was their impact and input into my life that gave life to this book.

INTRODUCTION

The towering evergreens lining the trail now blocked out the few remaining rays of sunshine. I began to feel chilly. My pace quickened, yet no matter how fast I walked, I was losing to the darkness.

Panic began to grip me.

I had come to this pristine, natural setting as a guest conference speaker. After dinner it seemed like a good idea for me to set out from my cabin on a short walk. Now, surrounded by gray sky and the silhouette of a dark forest, I could see I had made a poor choice. I visualized the retreat center I had left 20 minutes ago. It was so secluded that just 50 yards from the door, I looked back and couldn't see its rustic wood siding. How could I expect to see it, much less find it, now in the dark?

My first impulse was to run. Then I realized that if I took off in the wrong direction, I would really be in trouble. The back of my neck felt wet with sweat. Simply to stop and think seemed to be the smartest thing to do, rather than wandering in doubt.

I saw in front of me the outline of a steep hill, which was impossible to climb. I was stuck. Following my instincts, I decided to retrace my steps. I turned around, my mind racing. I did remember turning off the trail several minutes earlier. If I could find that turn, I might be able to return safely. It was one scrap of nervous hope I had left. I kept going, one foot scraping the trail in front of the other, walking, hoping in the dark.

I couldn't shake the anxiety or my imagination. As a kid, I often created frightful, make-believe creatures of the shrubs and bushes around our home. Now, as a 45-year-old man groping in the woods, the child inside me was alive. As the temperature dropped, my fear rose. I kept walking. Had I made the right decision?

Do the following words sound familiar?

Help—I'm lost.

I've blown it again.

I should have made the other choice.

Why did I rush into this?

I could have saved myself a whole lot of grief, energy, and pain had I made a better decision.

If you've ever found yourself on a dark trail, lost and afraid; if you've ever regretted a choice and wished you had it to do all over again; if you're tired of making poor decisions that leave you feeling drained, frustrated, and angry—choices that cause you to lose time, money, and a rare good night's sleep—then I want to share a three-part secret:

1. Life includes eight critical decisions everyone must make.
2. How you respond to each of these will determine your direction, happiness, and ultimate fulfillment in life.
3. Wherever you find yourself in life—regardless of age, occupation, previous setbacks, still-unresolved questions, or unfulfilled dreams—change is possible, beginning with your next decision.

I wrote this book because I believe nothing is more important in life than how you and I make decisions.

I speak from experience. When I was 15 years old, I was a bag boy at our hometown grocery store and saved $150 to purchase a 1946 Chevy Coupe. It was gorgeous, without one scratch. I didn't yet know how to drive, so the car sat in the garage, waiting for that magic day when I received my license. That day came too soon. One afternoon when no one was home, I decided to take my car for a short drive. I climbed in, shut the door, and revved the engine. Then I began backing it out. I looked out the rear window, turned sharply—and wiped out the left side of the car and the garage door. I've regretted that day, that decision, ever since. Yet it was not the only poor choice I would like to have back.

During college I worked as a service station attendant. One of my customers entertained me with stories about people who had made great fortunes investing in silver mines. He asked me if I would like to invest in a new mining venture. Within 24 hours I had withdrawn my total savings and purchased stock. I was so excited, so sure I would become rich, that I convinced some friends to invest. A few years later the mining company went broke, and we lost all our investments. Though I regretted losing my own money, I felt worse about my friends and how I had influenced them.

Years later a friend asked me to sign a guarantee on a loan he needed to make a business deal. (He was known to get excited about developing deals; then, before they produced, he would turn to a new project and abandon the old one.) I made the mistake of signing a three-year note for a man who had one year of staying power. After he walked away from this project, I had to pay off the last two years of the note. My friend was embarrassed by the ordeal, and we no longer have much of a friendship. If I had told him "No, I won't guarantee your note," we would likely be better friends today.

These and other poor decisions have brought me worry, frustration, and even some sorrow. Like the naive choice to walk along an unknown trail at dusk, these decisions have ushered me down a road of self-doubt and defeat. But something has happened along my life's trail that has surprised me: my unwise decisions have not brought defeat, but a new beginning. On the other side of the sign marked "Dead End" are the words "Keep Living."

By wisely making eight critical lifetime decisions, you can keep living and keep growing the rest of your life. You will learn principles, timeless truths that can help you discover new confidence, direction, and drive. In each chapter you'll see that the truths resulting from these eight decisions are things you can start applying *today*.

You can dramatically improve the quality of your life when you improve your decision-making skills—like a good decision I made to help a neighbor. Years ago, as I rode my bicycle through our neighborhood, I noticed a man shoveling a space for a new driveway. I climbed off my bike and asked him if I could help. He said, "Sure," and handed me a shovel.

All afternoon I labored under the hot sun until the concrete was poured and the job finished. The neighbor pulled out his wallet and asked, "What do I owe you?"

"I don't want any money—I just wanted to help you," I replied.

He was surprised, and from that day on he was a real friend. The decision I made to help this man taught me one of the greatest joys of living—that of helping others.

With a realistic, positive understanding of life's responsibilities, you can respond to challenges and roadblocks with maturity and wisdom. Instead of reacting to situations in a forced manner, you can respond with forethought and calm, free to be the person God designed you to be.

I'm not sure any of us fully "arrives." The moment I start to feel, "I've made it," along comes a situation, another important decision, that makes me realize I don't have all the answers. But I do have eight important milestones that serve as a compass to help me make other decisions.

Let me give you a sneak preview of the questions that deal with these eight key decisions as they mark out our journey in this book.

1. Because people shape your character, **Who will you call "friend"?**

When I was a young man, someone told me, "You should make friends now with people you would like to grow old with." I was too young to understand why this was important, but the idea holds a powerful ring of truth. Twenty-five years later, I can say it was some of the best advice I've ever received. The people you choose to "hang out" with determine the kind of person you'll become.

2. Because a good start is so important, **Where will you live?**

The view from the condominium window faced the point where the Noosa River joined the Pacific Ocean in a flowing ribbon of blue water. I could see the fishing fleet take to sea and return home at night with its catch. On the fringes of this real-life picture of paradise, palm trees swayed in the breeze. I thought, "This could be my home." But some very permanent decisions I had already made stood between me and fulfilling this dream. They're probably some of the same considerations you may have faced. Today, even though I'm 12,000 miles from those enticing palms, and even though rain and cold lurk outside my living room window, I wouldn't live any place other than where I'm sitting right now. I'm where I want to be today because of a decision I made many years ago. When you decide the type of lifestyle you want, where you live becomes a much easier decision.

3. Because nothing works until you do, **What will you do for a living?**

You will probably spend 100,000 hours—almost one-third of your entire life—in some kind of work. Is it any wonder that people who hate their jobs are some of the most miserable people? How do some people find the perfect fit with their jobs?

It's no coincidence they're confident and assured of their identity! I remember the day when this truth hit me. You never find a job that perfectly fits you, but you can fit yourself to the job. Folks who learn this great truth learn to love their jobs.

People who always look for a perfect job never find it. Those special individuals who seem to fit their jobs so well are ones who have chosen a job that fits their skills, and then learned to adapt to the job.

4. Because it doesn't grow on trees, **How will you handle money?**

A successful businessman was speaking to a young man about finances. "I've had a lot of money in my life, but it's never had me."

What did he mean? Maybe it's that money can be a benefit without enslaving you. I know some wonderful people who have discovered this truth. One pastor told me, "My wife and I have all the money we need to retire with financial dignity. We never pastored a large church or received a large salary. We've just planned 40 years for our retirement."

Another friend has substantial wealth but lives modestly in an average home and enjoys driving a pickup truck. He has a true understanding of money, because he's not hooked on it. These folks are proof of the axiom "It's not how much you have—it's what you do with it that determines your true wealth."

5. Because sooner or later you'll be tested, **How will you deal with temptation?**

I know a person who, when he was four years old, found his friend's plastic horse and liked it so much that he put it in his pocket. When he was five he took a candy bar from the grocery store and put it in his pocket. Today, 40 years later, he's a successful doctor. Yet when he goes shopping and sees something he wants, he sometimes feels like reaching for a "five-finger discount" without visiting the cashier. He remains confused about where his urges to steal come from, and he's still terrified that he might someday give into them. He's miserable and thinks he can't do anything about it. I would like to show him and you how to deal with temptations before they lead to trouble.

6. Because challenges are inevitable, **How will you respond to adversity?**

I remember leaving Anaheim Stadium with my team down seven to nothing. But my real discouragement waited up the road. After driving to the hotel, I pulled into the parking lot, got out, and then saw another car. Three men jumped out, one with a shotgun. I started running. I had taken three steps when the gun exploded and the pellets hit my back. Somehow I managed to keep running. The next few minutes and hours became a blurry nightmare—an all-too-real reminder that in a crisis you don't have time to think, only time to respond. And if it's a life-and-death situation you're facing, as this was, you may not get a second chance.

Somewhere between the gunshot and the stretcher, I promised myself I would never pass the opportunity to tell others why it's so critical to make wise decisions before you face them.

7. Because you're only human, **What will you do when your decisions fail?**

I was speaking with a woman at church during the greeting time of the worship service. When I asked, "How are you?" she said, "Just great."

From the clear look in her eyes and her warm handshake, I could tell she meant what she said. Her attitude surprised me, since I knew she was in the middle of a major turmoil. She's one of a host of people I've met who have learned that when your decisions fail, you can still control your response to life's circumstances. You can and will, because sooner or later, even your best efforts won't be enough. When you decide what you will do *when* (not if) your decisions fail, you're preparing yourself to face these moments. (If you're like me, you'll have plenty of opportunity to practice!) You'll find future decision-making much easier, because having a plan for handling a failed decision helps you make the next decision with confidence.

8. Because you can have only one boss in life, **Who's in charge of your life?**

Finally, we come to the heart of what really motivates us not to react to life in panic, but to respond out of confidence and strength. It has nothing to do with superior intellect, personality, or skill. It's the simplest but most challenging choice in life. This decision can take you far, if you're willing to admit you need help.

That brings me back to the story of being lost in the woods. After stumbling along the trail for a while, I came to a fork in the road. Neither path seemed to offer much security, but I chose the right one. Several minutes later, I saw the lights of the retreat center through the trees. I tried to stroll nonchalantly into the lodge, hoping no one would know my heart was pounding with nervous relief. I really don't think I fooled anyone.

Today, years later, the lesson of that dark night is still dawning on me: just as I was lost in the woods trying to find my way, many folks stumble around frustrated and anxious because they've failed to develop a strategy of living based on decisions they've already made. There is a better way.

Like the domino effect, learning how to make these eight key decisions can topple indecision, impulsiveness, or whatever else keeps you from making the best choices and reaching your dreams.

1 WHO WILL YOU CALL "FRIEND"?

NOTHING IN LIFE TAKES THE PLACE of a true friend. A friend will be a rock you can cling to when the storms of life try to pull you under. A friend will share your joys. A friend adds glory to your victories and takes some of the sting out of your defeats. A friend brings out the nobility within you. A friend accepts your shortcomings and praises your strengths. And when you get too big for your britches, a true friend will remind you that humility is the best prescription for pride.

If you know someone who matches this description, you're blessed. Most people enjoy many acquaintances but few friends. When the kinds of friendships people want so much don't develop and grow, they often settle for relationships that fall short of the intimacy, loyalty, and satisfaction they really want.

Is it possible to get beyond disappointments and build high-quality, lasting friendships? Yes! But it takes effort that most people aren't willing to make.

WHAT KIND OF FRIENDS DO YOU WANT?

I was 17 years old. I had just graduated from high school and was looking forward to college. For eight hours a day I worked at Beeson's Chevron service station in Lewiston, Idaho. Each day a parade of humanity drove in for a fill-up. One of the most memorable customers was Jim Roark. At least once a week he wheeled his new Oldsmobile up to the pump. Jim had everything I wanted: a new house, a nice wife and family, new clothes—not to mention the car of my dreams!

Part of Jim's job was to collect on overdue bills. His territory covered some of the roughest elements in Lewiston. One day, as I checked the oil in his car, Jim looked over at me and said, "How would you like to ride around with me tomorrow as I make some calls?"

"That would be great—-I'd like that very much," I said excitedly. *Why was Jim Roark taking an interest in me?* I wondered. The only reason I came up with was the fact that I was a local weightlifting champion and enjoyed a fairly good reputation as a boxer.

The next day I sat in Jim's Oldsmobile, and for two hours I learned how an acquaintance grows into a friendship. Jim showed an interest in me. He asked about what things I enjoyed doing, where I was headed beyond high school, and what I wanted out of life. And he was a great listener. When he dropped me off at my house, I was sad to say goodbye. Jim made sure we spent more times together. A lot more. Over the years, Jim Roark has defined the word "friend" for me, because by making me his friend, he showed me how to be a friend to others.

And that's the secret: *If you want to enjoy good friendships that last a lifetime, spot the admirable qualities in others that you want for yourself.*

Jim Roark had all the qualities of a lifelong friend.

1. A solid character built on trust

People of character are people you can trust. They keep their word. They keep commitments. They are dependable. Like all good personal traits, their trustworthiness wears off on you if you're around them long enough.

A true friend will lift you to a higher plane. You'll be able to spot people who would cause you to stumble and compromise your character. Friends who are unable to resist temptation are anxious to justify their own behavior by compromising others. A real friend doesn't encourage you to do anything that makes you feel guilty. *Can you name the person in your life whose solid character inspires and motivates you to be your best?* This is the kind of person you want to hold on to.

2. A willingness to set and achieve worthy goals

Like solid character, success is contagious. If you hang out with ambitious people who attain worthy goals, you'll do the same. Your shared ambition can grow into mutual support that forms the basis of a great friendship. As you share your decisions and plans, you draw strength and courage from each other.

The opposite is just as true. If you hang out with losers, you'll soon act and think like a loser. These people are generally easy to spot, because they're basically takers. They draw off your energy and rarely give anything back to the relationship. *When you think of people who want to "give back" out of friendship, what faces come to mind?*

3. An eagerness to learn

Find someone who loves new ideas, and you'll discover someone who loves to learn and grow. For me, a desire to learn is synonymous with friendship, and in particular, a man named Ralph Bruksos. Ralph is a trainer who leads executive reading and thinking groups. Once every four to eight weeks he meets for all or most of a day with people who have read a chosen book. I've participated in some of these groups. The only things greater than the ideas, insights, and mental stimulation are the people. Many who participate in these meetings have become great friends. The learning and sharing in these sessions creates a great foundation for friendship.

4. An ability to speak the truth in love

If you let someone really know you, he or she will eventually see your mistakes. This is when a true friend comes to the fore. A true friend will point out the folly of a planned course of action, because he or she really cares about you and wants the best for you. A friend won't just tell you what you want to hear. Rather, if he or she sees you heading in a direction that could be harmful to you and your future, he or she will tell you about it.

Abraham Lincoln appointed some of his bitter enemies to his cabinet because he knew they would tell him the truth. He had learned that knowing the truth is the only way to self-improvement. An enemy who tells you the truth is better than a friend who flatters, but a friend who tells the truth is the best of all. When you have friends who tell you the truth, you increase your opportunity to grow and become a better person.

When I was still in school, Jim Roark offered to take me shopping for some new clothes. He knew I didn't have the best fashion judgment. Because he cared for me, he spoke the truth in love. He taught me how important it was to dress well. Today, I still thank him for his courage to confront and his desire to care. *Do you know someone who has both the boldness and sensitivity to tell you the truth in love?*

5. A willingness to laugh—especially at yourself

I'm the only person I know who has backed his or her car out of the garage without opening the garage door. Today I know I have friends in the world, because they're the ones still laughing with me at this legendary feat of mine. Good friends know how to laugh. They know that sooner or later each of us fails and that the only thing we *can* do, sometimes, is laugh. True friends help you to laugh at yourself. They can laugh *with* you, not *at* you. Can you hear the laugh of that special someone who would love to be laughing with you right now? Such a person makes this proverb real: "Laughter is the shortest distance between two people, two *friends.*"

6. A heart for God

Each of us is born with an innate desire to know our Creator. Alex Haley's book *Roots* stirred our country's imagination as it traced the ancestry of a black family in America. Like the characters in *Roots*, most of us want to know where we came from and where we're going. I've always been intrigued by the fact that people with a heart for God have decided to seek Him out to learn more about their history and their future. Their spiritual journey becomes a focal point in their lives. When you're around people like this, they challenge you to think about the spiritual dimension in your own life. Not only that, but people committed to seek-

> IF YOU WANT TO ENJOY GOOD FRIENDSHIPS THAT LAST A LIFETIME, YOU MUST EXHIBIT THE ADMIRABLE QUALITIES YOU SEE IN OTHERS.

ing God tend to possess the qualities we've just discussed. Do all or most of these qualities come together in anyone you know? What would it look like to build a friendship with this person?

THE OTHER HALF OF THE SECRET

If you think you've found the secret to building good, lasting friendships, I have news for you: you're only halfway home. That little extra effort that most people don't want to make, that small but infinite distance between *wishing* for a friend and actually *having* a friend is wrapped up in one tiny Old Testament verse: "A man who has friends must himself be friendly" (Prov. 18:24). Translation: To have a friend, first *be* a friend. If you want to enjoy good friendships that last a lifetime, you must exhibit the admirable qualities you see in others.

When I was a boy, my parents often invited friends to our house for Sunday dinner after church. Some days they would beat my mother to the punch and invite *us* to dinner. No wonder these people became lifetime friends. We went to church together, played together, and at times cried together. Miles could not separate what years of wonderful get-togethers had built. My mother still exchanges letters with these and other friends that go back to high school days. These relationships have been a source of comfort in sorrow and have provided an unbroken thread of love in the sometimes disorderly tapestry of life.

My mother knew the extra effort it takes to build friendships. Instead of wondering if others were thinking of *her*, she would say, "I've been thinking about you. Would you like to come to dinner this Sunday?" Instead of wishing someone would write *her*, she would pick up a pen and write to *them*. No matter how busy your world is, you can help build a friendship in just five minutes. That's how long it takes to make a phone call, write a postcard, invite someone to coffee, or simply tell him or her, "I've been thinking about you." A few minutes of caring can turn into years of satisfaction.

When I was in my mid-20s, my wife, Darlys, and I moved

to a new town. On our first Sunday at a new church we met John Wordsworth. He was an established businessman and an outstanding Christian. I quickly saw that he had many of the qualities I wanted to develop. I decided I wanted to be his friend.

John taught a Sunday School class for young married couples. As Darlys and I became faithful members, we volunteered to teach John's class when he was out of town.

Eventually we became coteachers and taught together for 14 years. Darlys and I looked after John's kids when he and his wife, Vi, were away, and John and I became golfing partners. Off the course we prayed, laughed, and cried together.

My friendship with John grew for more than 25 years, until he reached the end of his earthly journey. Much of the reason is because I saw something in John I liked: loyalty. I learned from my parents not to simply admire loyalty but to practice it. Not only did I want to have a friend—I chose to *be* a friend. As a result of this commitment, I learned what real friendship is—two people choosing to give to each other out of mutual care and respect.

What Goes Around . . .

Do certain television commercials stick in your mind? For some reason I still remember the one that showed two women talking in a derogatory manner about their "friend" Jan. All of a sudden, Jan walked into the room. The woman doing the hatchet job on Jan smiled at her and gushed, "Oh—hi, Jan!"

This ad taught me an important principle: good friends don't speak negatively about each other. If you say anything at all, why not say something encouraging to build up the other person? This is what it means to be loyal.

As with anything you do to build a friendship, you *choose* to be loyal. The choice to be loyal is really quite simple when you remember the principle that whatever you say about others tends to come back around. The mark of loyalty is that your words of praise and support for others will be the same words people use to describe *you*.

The Fat's in the Fire!

Just how important is loyalty? In any lasting friendship, loyalty isn't an option—it's a lifesaver. In frontier times, people often cooked with lard, which would sometimes catch on fire. Perhaps this is how the phrase "the fat's in the fire" got started. To old-timers, this meant that a problem or emergency was at hand. If you want to be a good friend, be there when "the fat's in the fire."

A nugget from Proverbs contains a lifetime of truth: "A friend loves at all times, and a brother is born for adversity" (Prov. 17:17). Sooner or later someone you know will face adversity. Where will you be when the call for help goes out, when the fire rages and the heat is on? Will you give that little extra effort that comes with being a friend?

Darwin "Cub" Grimm taught me the truth of this principle. My father died when I was 17 years old. My mother and two younger sisters moved from Clarkston, Washington, to Spokane to stay with family. I was on my own. Cub was my weightlifting coach and a friend from church. He rented me a room in his basement and a place at his dinner table. Most important, he gave me a piece of his heart and shared his life with me. His acts of friendship and strength of character helped shape my life. He came beside me during a time of confusion and struggle and helped guide me from despair to victory. His counsel and friendship turned the course of my life. He was a friend who put action to the words of friendship.

WHEN GOD BECOMES YOUR FRIEND

At an early age I personally came to know the God of the Bible. This is the God who loves and accepts you and me unconditionally through Jesus Christ. I can't presume that you have met this God. But I feel confident sharing with you how my life changed for the better when I began to see God as my Friend. When I saw that He is interested in walking beside me through all of life, that He loves me and promises never to leave me, I began to know I was loved. I began to feel secure with Him. As I spent time with Him in prayer and listened for

His direction, He became less of a mysterious Being and more of an intimate, personal Friend.

And I found something else. Although human friendships are wonderful, no earthly relationships can fill your heart the way God can. He knows you and understands you better than anyone. He is not limited to time and space as you and I are. He can be with you anywhere and at anytime.

If you want a friend, be a friend—to God. And you will be drawn into a relationship that will change your life. As the Bible says, "Draw near to God and He will draw near to you" (James 4:8).

The Choice Is Up to You

I hope this chapter has helped you identify people in your life who define the word "friend." Whether you've known them for years or only a few months, think of the opportunities before you that can begin to unfold as you answer these questions:

1. What specific qualities do you look for in a friendship? Make a list of those traits, and beside each trait write the name of someone you know who demonstrates that quality. Based on your discoveries, take steps to improve your friendships with these folks. If your list is short, you may need to broaden your search for friendships.

2. What extra little effort would make your existing friendships stronger or help develop new relationships? For each friend your strategy may be different, but the basic commitment is the same. Sometime between reading this sentence and the getting up from your chair, you should choose how to be a friend to some and a better friends to others.

One time I decided to list all the perfect people I had known in my life. It turned out to be a short list—mine was the only name! Then I got honest, and no one was on the list. There have been times in my life when I thought I had met perfect people, but then I discovered that there were only better actors and actresses in the world.

When you get to know the real person, you won't just be

admiring the wrapper—you'll appreciate the genuine contents. Friendship is not about being perfect. It's about understanding and forgiving. Perhaps the greatest gift a friend can give is accepting you as you really are with all of your imperfections.

In fact, I can't think of a better gift you or I could give another person. Unconditional acceptance is the ultimate expression of love. To be a real friend, we need to accept others where they are in their life journey.

One Sunday I was speaking in a growing church of 3,000 attendees. I asked the pastor what he thought was the secret of the congregation's growth. He replied that they "just accept people as they are." In addition to its being an important part of a growing church, it's also the secret of a growing friendship.

Author Mark Twain once said that the Bible tells us to love our enemies—and that just for practice we should try it on our friends.

TAKING THE FIRST STEP

● Decide to place a high priority on developing friendships.

● List three ways you can be a better friend to others today:

1. _____

2. _____

3. _____

Describe actions you can take to improve the quality and quantity of your friendships:

_____

_____

_____

_____

_____

An old proverb says a journey of a thousand miles starts with the first step. Start walking the friendship journey today.

2 WHERE WILL YOU LIVE?

BETWEEN THE TIME I WAS 22 and 35 years old, my life changed dramatically. I went from being a single person to a happily married individual who enjoyed raising two children. At work, I went from making $325 a month as a personnel consultant to being a well-paid vice president responsible for a budget of a quarter of a billion dollars, 1,000 employees, and multimillion-dollar loans. And during those years, something else played a huge role in my growth: I moved from Spokane, Washington, to Seattle. This change of geography, home, neighborhood, and friends proved to be one of the most important choices of my life. As I look back, I can see a truth that's too obvious, too pivotal to ignore: When you choose where you live, you discover and affirm the values that will mold and shape your life.

> WHEN YOU CHOOSE WHERE YOU LIVE, YOU DISCOVER AND AFFIRM THE VALUES THAT WILL MOLD AND SHAPE YOUR LIFE.

Let me share a few things that most people overlook about this extremely important matter.

Someone Who Believes in You

Did you know that God is interested in where you live? The Bible tells us the story of a family who moved because God told them to. The man's name was Abram. He lived in Haran, where God said to him one day, "Get out of your country, From your family And from your father's house, To a land that I will show you. I will make you a great nation; I will bless you And make your name great; And you shall be a blessing. I will bless those who bless you, And I will curse him who curses you; And in you all the families of the earth shall be blessed" (Gen. 12:1-3). The Bible says Abram did what God told him to do—he moved. Abram obeyed, and God fulfilled His promise, as Abram eventually became the father of the Israelite and Arab nations.

We don't always hear God's voice as clearly as Abram did. But God does call people to live in specific places. Famed missionary David Livingstone felt a desire to take the gospel to Africa. In so doing, he gave up a promising medical career in England. He knew God had a specific place for him to serve, and moving to that place changed his life. How "at home" did Livingstone feel on the Dark Continent? When he died they buried his heart in Africa and shipped the rest of his body back to England.

Have you considered asking God to direct your decision to move? Recently I spoke with a young man named Brian Helstrom. Years ago, his ancestors had immigrated to the United States from Sweden. He was moving his young family back to his ancestors' native homeland to start a new congregation for the Church of the Nazarene. Recently I read of a Cambodian pastor in Long Beach, California, who was leaving a thriving church to start a new congregation in Cambodia.

The all-important decision of when and where to move can come at any time in life. Bruce Kennedy was in his 50s when he resigned as chief executive officer of Alaska Airlines. He and his wife moved to a third-world country to help children learn to read.

Each of these people had at least one thing in common with Abram: because they knew God loved them, they could totally trust Him with the decision of "Where will I live?" When you realize God loves you as much as he loved Abram, this question of "Where?" becomes a joyful surrender: *Lord, by giving You complete control of my life, I surrender my right to determine where I'll live. Therefore, I'll go where you want me to go. I'll be what you want me to be.*

Just think: because He loves you, God no doubt has

something very special planned for your life. But you'll find it only if you're willing to go where He sends you. As you give this matter to God, He'll meet you in your decision. God has equipped you with a logical mind to help you think through big decisions. If "Where to move?" is something you're asking, even if it's a question still waiting down the road, you can ask practical, specific questions that will help you make a wise choice consistent with God's values and the wonderful things He has planned for you.

FIVE KEYS TO FINDING THE BEST LOCATION

It may happen suddenly or evolve over time. Sooner or later, however, you will probably face the possibility of moving. It could be for education, a new job, or a new lifestyle. Whatever the reason, you've targeted a particular region, city, or town. You've seen the area and perhaps even spread out the classified ads and scanned the listings under "Homes to Buy," or "Apartments to Rent." You are excited, cautious, and maybe a little unsure as you ponder, *Where would be the best place to live?*

Without a set of objective criteria to evaluate your options, you might succumb to changing emotions, erroneous first impressions, or impatience. I've seen these and other influences blind people from finding the neighborhood, district, or actual dwelling that best fits them.

Over the years I've developed what I call "Five Keys to Finding the Location That Fits You." For years I scribbled these five questions across note pads and on the backs of envelopes. Before you make a final decision on where to move, consider the following five suggestions:

1. Consider the stability of the neighborhood.

Do the people in this area own their homes? It's important to know if people own their homes, because a healthy community will have widespread home ownership. Homeowners have a great stake in their community. Usually they're families who've invested not only money but their time, effort, and values in neighborhood schools, businesses, and the image of the place they call home. It's something you'll see in nicely mown lawns, freshly painted houses, and overall friendliness of the people.

How do you find the percentage of home ownership in a particular area? The real estate industry publishes an affordability index in each community. It figures the percentage of people who can buy their own homes. This index takes the average price of a house and compares it with the average family income. It then computes the number of people in the marketplace who could, if they managed their finances well, afford to buy a house. Your bank, real estate broker, real estate multiple listing office, or local library should be able to give you this information.

2. Consider schools.

What kind of involvement is there in parent-teacher groups? If you have, or expect to have, school-aged children, you'll want to know the general parent interest in local education. Schools supported by a broad base of parents will be better than schools where parents are out of touch and uninvolved. And don't stop with elementary, middle, or secondary schools. Ask, "Is continuing education available? Are there vocational, skill, and craft classes for adult learners, the elderly, and people who want to learn for fun? Does the local educational system have a good reputation? Do its graduates return and give back to the community?"

3. Consider churches.

How important is it to you to find a worshiping community affiliated with your present denomination or tradition? Pick up a telephone directory and scan the yellow pages. Read the religion section in your local newspaper. If you know Christian friends in the area, ask them about this.

By asking people, reading, and observing, you can learn more about the moral and spiritual climate of a place than you might have thought. You'll be able to have some idea about whether this community will help you grow and become a better person. By then you may have learned more than the names of local congregations. You may have discovered who's winning the battle for the hearts and lives of the people. These discoveries will help you answer the question, "Am I better off looking for a worshiping community where I will be secure, or one that will challenge me to make this a better place to live?"

4. Consider the economy.

Who and what are driving the business development in this community? What is the job base? What's the unemployment level, and the level of people engaged in productive work? Newspapers and business reports will reveal the area's economic strengths and weaknesses. Think twice about a community that relies on one employer. A mix of strong businesses usually creates a more stable economic climate.

Why is this important to you even if you're not in business? The dollars that are being earned and spent ultimately impact prices, other companies, and other jobs —including yours.

5. Consider safety.

Who's running City Hall? It's easy to take police and fire protection for granted until your own life, family, or home is in danger. What is the track record of the public safety departments? Call the specific offices and ask for their crime and fire reports. Local service clubs, block watch programs, and citizen action groups will gladly tell you what's happening if you ask.

At times in life, God's blessings emerge in a way that's impossible to ignore. When I was 27, I unexpectedly received a lucrative job offer. The offer was tempting: more money, more status, and more responsibility. But I would need to move to what seemed like a "far country." Even with this drawback, I didn't know how I could say "No" to such an excellent career move.

I sat down, took a deep breath and then took a bit of my own medicine: I looked at the job offer in light of each of these five key points. After I finished my investigation, the decision was easy. Instead of moving I chose to stay in Seattle.

The next year, our community was picked as the "Most Livable City in America." I've never regretted the decision to stay.

THE IMPORTANT ROLE OF FAMILY IN CHOOSING A LOCATION

If you're single, these five considerations about where to live can give you an excellent opportunity to consider what you really value. If you're married, and especially if you have children, the possibility of moving presents you with an added responsibility and opportunity to see God at work in your life.

I started life in Pullman, a small agriculture-based town surrounded by rolling wheat fields in eastern Washington. It was a beautiful area of rich farms and down-to-earth people. My grandparents and many of my aunts and uncles lived in nearby Spokane. The memories of drinking hot chocolate, sledding in the snow, fresh-baked cookies, and summer fishing trips created a feeling of love and security that has sustained me through the years. The guidance, security, and identity I received from my parents and siblings showed me the goodness of family. Their love was the tangible, human expression of God's own love. Raising my own family has only deepened this conviction. I believe more than ever that anything that can be done to strengthen families is a high priority on God's agenda. Sometimes, as with Abram, that strengthening comes through a move. I realize family relationships are tricky, and loving your relatives can take extra effort. If, however, you value your family relationships, you'll value the chance to minimize the miles that separate you.

Through the years, many family members from my wife's family and my own have moved to within an hour's drive of where we live. After countless times of rich conversation, laughter, and even shared sorrows, I wish they had made the move sooner. Every time I have welcomed them with a hug or said good-bye with a wave, I've come home to the warm thought that it's great to have family nearby. Life is more pleasant when you can share it with the ones you love.

Suppose your possible move takes you away from family.

What then? When I was young, I felt I should work for a company that offered me a job in Tacoma, Washington. This was almost 250 miles away from my home and family. The only people I knew in Tacoma were a young couple I had met in college. The man pastored a small church in the city. Since I had no family in Tacoma, this caring man and his wife reached out to me. They became my family.

Wherever I've been, I've found that the Church has provided a loving, extended family for people who've had to leave their own families behind. Believe me, nothing can take the place of your own family. Yet caring, Christian friends are God's living reminders of people back home who think of you in their prayers, their letters, and their care packages!

WHY A LONG-TERM COMMITMENT CREATES A LIFETIME OF SATISFACTION

Statistics show that the average American will move seven to eight times in his or her life. Does the idea of pulling up stakes, sinking new roots, and then repeating the same process every 10 years seem appealing? If you're committed to a company or the military, moves can't be helped. But think of what it would mean to live in one area for 20 or 30 years. I believe we find major benefits to living a long time in an area we enjoy. Making a long-term commitment to anything positive is valuable to our lives.

For the past 25 years my family has lived near Seattle. I can say without question this has been an excellent decision. We've been tempted to move several times. Each time we said "No" to that possibility, we actually said "Yes" to our growing friendships with neighbors, church friends, business associates, and others we have come to cherish. The advantages of "staying put" become benefits. You can grow to enjoy and count on favorite sights, stores, and hangouts. You know where to find the library, your favorite restaurant, a good cup of coffee, or a beautiful sunset.

One day I was sitting by the pool at a condominium in Noosa, Australia. The palm trees were swaying gently in the breeze, and the temperature was a balmy 82 degrees. I knew that at the moment rain was probably falling in Seattle.

Why don't I move to Noosa? I thought. For all its natural beauty and appeal, I *didn't* move because I feel so comfortable where I live! Noosa is a great place to visit in my memories (and I hope to physically visit there again), but Woodinville, Washington, is where I want to live. I agree with Dorothy in *The Wizard of Oz*—there's no place like home. If God should ever want me to move, I'm willing to go. But just between you and me, I hope I can stay here until I make that ultimate move —to heaven.

Your decision to move might be filled with questions and concerns you can't answer until you're finally in your new place. A second source of satisfaction comes years later when you look back and say, "I'm glad we stayed and made this place our home."

TAKE ACTION! THREE STEPS FOR MOVING IN THE RIGHT DIRECTION

Where are you when it comes to moving? How well do you like the place where you live? Have recent opportunities caused you to think a move may be in your future? Are you looking to stay in one place for the next one, two, ten, or twenty years?

Whether moving is a distant thought or a looming reality, you can do several things today to help you appreciate the place God has for you. Ask yourself the following questions.

Can I learn to be content where I am?

Most people spend too much time worrying about where they would like to live and not enough time enjoying where they are. Have you thought about looking for ways to accomplish your dreams right where you are? You've probably heard the saying "Bloom where you're planted." What would it mean to nourish the "soil" of your job, your family, your community involvement? What would it look like to see your roots grow deeper so that the fruit of your life could fully come into bloom?

Are there ways to improve my world?

Wherever you are, you could make a wonderful contribution to your community, your church, your company, or your home. Sometime recently you have probably said, "If only . . ." or "What if . . ." The words that complete these sentence starters are the wishes you desire to fulfill. What's keeping you from acting on these dreams?

In what direction am I going?

Before you move, ask, "Am I running from something or moving to something? Will changing locations solve a problem, or am I trying to avoid solving a problem that's in front of me?" Don't let false motivations con you. You could save yourself a world of headaches and rediscover the place you already call home by discovering "right here" is where you belong.

When, and if, you move, have a plan! You can improve the quality and ultimate success of your decision-making with a thoughtful plan. As you consider all the options, sort the pros and cons, pray, and realize God is interested in your well-being. Know He will work through the goals you set and the plans you make.

Taking the First Step

Decide today that you will live wherever God wants you to be. Decide to be where you are while you are there. Decide to research a potential move carefully and make the decision prayerfully.

Whenever I am confronted with a decision to move, I will

_____

_____

_____

Be thankful for wherever you are now. And the next time you decide to move, you won't make the journey alone. The God who moved Abram goes with you wherever you live.

3 WHAT WILL YOU DO FOR A LIVING?

"I WANT TO CHANGE JOBS!"

This is a frequent confession. Unhappiness in our work frustrates us, and too often it controls us. With the right strategy, you can master your work and avoid the ulcers and constant stress that destroys people, families, and careers. The approach I want to share with you revolves around the goodness of work and several basic assumptions:

You'll spend up to 60 percent of your life at some kind of job. If you enjoy what you're doing, you'll enjoy life.

Your work is a major source of income. If you're well suited to your job, you'll be more productive and will earn more.

Your work gives you a big piece of your identity. If what you do is matched to who you are, your sense of purpose and fulfillment will rise and possibly spread to other parts of your life.

The simplicity of these truths is the beauty of the plan I want to share with you. But first, let's spend a few minutes and see what so many have been missing.

DISCOVERING YOUR DESIGN AND DETERMINING YOUR PURPOSE

When I got married, I decided I should be able to fix anything that broke. I was the man, and every man knows how to work with tools. Things around our small apartment broke all the time. Every time a faucet handle came loose or a hinge fell off, I discovered I had not been born with a screwdriver in my hand! Pounding a two-inch nail was a major feat. Any more demanding fix-it task brought me to my knees.

My wife Darlys watched in shock. She had grown up on a farm in North Dakota, and her father was a master mechanic. Often she handed him tools on complicated repair jobs. Fixing something was second nature for her. When my efforts started to fall apart, she would offer a suggestion. This didn't help me. In fact, the more I knew what I was doing wrong, the more frustrated I became. Eventually I got so discouraged I gave up. Two days later I would come back to the squeaky door or the broken cup and see that Darlys had fixed it. I put my male ego on the shelf and did the wisest thing I could—I bought my wife some new tools!

We're all designed differently. You have a skill package that makes you gifted and unique. If you discover your skills and then package yourself to sell them in the marketplace, you'll enjoy your work. You'll be productive. And you'll see your sense of confidence and identity pay off in other areas of life.

How do you discover your unique design? First, gather information *before* you make any major decisions about work. As a personnel executive, I designed a simple self-inventory that has helped thousands of job applicants discover their qualities, talents, and interests. The inventory can do the same for you.

Step 1. On a scale of 1 to 10, with 1 being lowest and 10 being highest, rate yourself in the following nine areas listed on the chart on the next page.

Step 2. Write a list of your "success experiences" and accomplishments you felt good about in your past jobs.

Step 3. List "success experiences" that are not job related. Be sure to include childhood events. Why do these specific accomplishments have meaning to you? Write your observations and conclusions next to each one.

Step 4. Based on the exercises you listed, describe the type of activities that would bring you the most job satisfaction. What kind of job would incorporate these activities?

Step 5. Visit with a friend you respect. Ask him or her to review your answers and give you honest observations and suggestions. Do the same thing with your parents, relatives, teachers, or others you know well. What are the common themes, insights, suggestions, or comments you hear from these people?

Step 6. Realizing there's no "right" answer, write down your responses to these questions:

QUALITY	RATING									
	Low									High
	1	2	3	4	5	6	7	8	9	10
Mechanical Aptitude										
Analytical Skills										
Ability to Work Alone										
Ability to Build Friendships										
Capacity to Learn New Ideas										
Discipline										
Follow-through										
Integrity										
Health and Stamina										

- What did you learn about your interests?
- What did you learn about the kinds of jobs that fit those interests?

Targeting Your Career Objectives

The previous six steps can produce one of two insightful results. Your self-assessment may point you toward specific career goals or objectives, or you may find your career objectives have come out of seemingly insignificant decisions.

Let me give you four reasons I'm convinced your work future may be found in these "insignificant" choices.

My first major career decision took place in high school. In English class I had to write a theme about a profession. Since my uncle sold electric furnaces, I wrote about salespeople. As I wrote about Ike and thought about how neat he was, I could see myself in sales. Imagining myself in a particular role prepared me for that line of work. I realize now that I wasn't simply writing a theme paper—I was writing a story in which I would one day be the main character. In this "insignificant" moment I discovered my future profession.

Later I experienced a second moment of equal "insignificance." One Saturday morning while washing windows at a shoe store where I worked part-time as a teenager, I noticed a man walking to the clothing store next door, where he worked. I liked his suit and tie so much that as he strolled by, I told a woman I worked with, "Someday I'm going to dress like him."

She laughed and said, "I wouldn't count on that. It takes a lot of money for the kind of clothes he's wearing."

I didn't care what it cost. I was willing to pay the price and find a career that would allow me to dress as well as this man. Three years later I was fortunate to own three suits in my job as a salesperson for Telache Oil and Mining Company.

Maybe it's not so insignificant that I met Jim Roark, whom I mentioned earlier. Jim managed a branch of a small loan company in Lewiston, Idaho, and became one of my heroes. He had what I wanted: great people skills and his own office with a desk.

When I was 24, the company I worked for sent me to an eight-week self-improvement course with my wife, Darlys. The last night of the course, the speaker, Bill Cady, concluded the evening. When I heard him speak, it was as if God were speaking to me: "You could be a motivational speaker just like this man." That moment I decided I would do everything I could to fulfill this dream. Today, whenever I put on a suit coat and address an audience of 50 to 100 people, I ask myself, "What if I had neglected those 'insignificant' decisions? Where would I be now?"

God can and will speak to you through your significant talents and what might seem like life's insignificant moments. In God's eyes they're both important.

Targeting your career objectives is one of the most important things you can do if you're starting out. But what if you're already working and considering a job change?

GROWING WHERE YOU'RE PLANTED

Over the years, I've interviewed thousands of people who were looking for work. Most of them simply wanted to find a better job. The wanted an opportunity to grow and develop their skills. They wanted to have more fun, enjoy their job, find a better boss, earn more money, and do more meaningful things.

Although their motivations were generally good, something was wrong. Soon after these people changed jobs they became just as unhappy as they were in their former position. They were discontent because they never mastered their previous job before moving on. They hadn't learned a basic principle of work: life is a series of lessons. If you don't invest the time and effort to learn the lessons facing you *today,* you'll keep getting the same tests and failing them for the rest of your life.

However, by learning today's lessons today, you'll be ready to go on to some new material. I wish I had learned this lesson sooner than I did.

In high school I could bluff my way through the first semester of a Spanish class without learning much. I approached the second semester with the same carefree attitude. Toward the end of the semester, I faced the day of reckoning: the class had been designed on cumulative learning. Each step in learning Spanish was built on knowing the previous lesson. By the time I realized this, it was too late. It was the first class I ever failed, yet it taught me a lesson I've shared with unhappy employees itching for a change: *Until you've learned the lessons and passed the tests of where you are now, the only benefit you'll receive from changing jobs is a change of scenery.*

If you want to advance your career, instead of changing jobs, try to grow where you're planted. The wisdom of this principle is not found in immediate results, but in perseverance and patience. People who grow where they're planted discover the daily satisfaction of planting, cultivating, and weeding their particular "field." More times than not, the harvest of increased accomplishment, relationships, and earnings makes the patient person say, "I'm glad I stayed put, because otherwise I may have never discovered how good the growing conditions were right at my feet."

When is it right to change jobs? Based on years of observation, I believe it's not until you've mastered your current position. Only then will you be ready for new learning experiences. Have you learned everything you can at your present place of employment? Here are some questions that can help you answer this question:

1. Have you learned to support your boss wholeheartedly? You're never ready to change jobs until you've given your boss 100 percent of your support. 1 Tim. 6:1 says we should treat our bosses with total respect.

"But my boss is a jerk," you might say. This may be true. However, the boss is still the boss. Your job is not to change him or her. Your job is to do your best work so that you might change and grow. If you can learn to support a bad boss, you'll be much more effective supporting a good one. Just think of the alternative. If you don't learn this lesson, what will you do if your next boss is *worse*?

I remember being frustrated at work because people with

far less productivity were advancing faster and receiving better cooperation from our boss. Instead of steaming, I decided to surprise this supervisor I was having a difficult time working for. At an important meeting the next day I told this man, "I know we need to make some changes and I'll do whatever you want me to do."

He looked at me with surprise and said, "What do you think we ought to do?"

I told him my suggestions, and he said, "Let's do it!" It was interesting to notice that when *I* got on *his* team, *he* got on *my* team. From then on, we developed a great working relationship. What I thought were competing interests were now complementary strengths that built our sense of confidence in each other. Once I told my boss, "I support you," and backed my words up with action, my career grew and prospered.

2. How well do you discipline yourself and manage your time? One way to know you're ready for a new job is having learned to get maximum productivity in your current work. One day at a seminar I was leading, a woman said, "At my workplace we're supposed to take 15-minute breaks. In reality, everyone takes 25- to 30-minute breaks. After hearing you, I feel this is wrong. What should I do?"

I suggested that when her 15-minute break is up she go back to work. I saw her a few months later, and she told me she had done that. "At first, all my coworkers just looked at me strangely. Now they all go back to work on time."

Do you think this woman is ready to learn other lessons?

3. Do you maximize your productive time at work? Do you start working when you start getting paid? Do you prioritize your tasks and do the most important work first? Do you finish critical tasks before you leave work? Or do you leave things undone? We've each been given 24 hours in a day. How do you plan to use your time wisely?

Undiscovered Treasure, Undeveloped Potential

I once read about two brothers who went to work as young men in the paint department of a large manufacturing company. Each had similar skills and similar backgrounds. One brother spent all his spare time having fun. The second brother took night classes in accounting. He soon received a promotion and became a company accountant. In the meantime, he took all the management and self-improvement courses the company offered. And eventually this man, Harlow Curtis, became president of General Motors, the world's largest builder of automobiles—while his brother still worked in the paint department.

Have you taken advantage of all the educational opportunities your company offers? Have you mastered all the aspects of your job? If someone were to watch you work, would he or she say, "There's a real pro in action"?

If you're content to stay at your present level throughout the coming years, you may want to keep doing what you're doing. However, if you're interested in growing into a more challenging, more exciting, perhaps better-paying job, you may want to ask, "What skills do I need to reach that next level? How can I get there with my current skills?"

Several years ago the president of a large company hired me to conduct a series of videotaped interviews with the firm's executives. He wanted the company's employees to see and know these leaders "up close and personal," in hopes of building better trust and morale.

I asked each executive, "What have you done to further your education in your field?" Without exception, the higher the leader, the more he or she had chosen to know virtually everything about his or her field. Each person had risen to the top in the company by knowing more about the industry than anyone else. Each had experienced one of the great benefits of education—that learning expands one's opportunities. Increase your storehouse of knowledge, and you can't help but grow as an employee and as a person. Who can say "No" to an opportunity this good?

THE NEGLECTED ASSET

One of life's great mysteries is how intense preparation in one area of work can lead to opportunities in an unrelated

field. The people who have been able to understand and benefit from this truth are those who have learned how to stay
flexible. Sara liked to take care of people. As a girl, she often
went out of her way to be helpful to others. It's no surprise
that she eventually became a nurse. She gave her whole self to
nursing. By learning everything she could, by growing from
her mistakes, she became an outstanding nurse.

Sara's career seemed cut short when circumstances forced
her to move to a new town with no nursing opportunities.
She decided to try real estate. After several months of hard
work, she surpassed the income she had made as a nurse.
Sara's success wasn't that surprising when you consider the
nursing skills she brought to her new job: helpfulness, attention to detail, and a commitment to knowing her field inside
and out. The wonderful twist came when nursing opportunities opened back up and she returned to her first career love.

Sara's willingness to be flexible in her career paid huge
dividends. Flexibility is rooted in determination and a promise. Prov. 16:9 says, "A man's heart plans his ways, But the
LORD directs his steps." If you're committed to trusting and
following God's leadership, He will guide your career and provide give you opportunities you may have never dreamed
about. As Sara discovered, the key is learning to be flexible.

I'm sure that when James Dobson, founder and president
of Focus on the Family, was studying child development at
the University of Southern California, he never dreamed he
would one day become one of the world's best-known radio
speakers or the head of an international ministry dedicated to
strengthening the family. God had a plan for his life built on
cumulative learning. Dobson's experiences in education prepared him to write, deliver, and broadcast clear, dynamic mes-
sages about how to develop parenting skills. His career is just
one obvious reminder of how God may lead you in directions
you could never plan with your limited vision of the future.

By learning to be flexible today, you could save yourself
from an unexpected tragedy tomorrow. Rusty thought his job
as a timber worker would go on forever. He never foresaw the

day when lumber was priced out of the marketplace and the federal government passed legislation prohibiting logging on land inhabited by the endangered northern spotted owl. Through no fault of his own, Rusty found himself out of work. He could not afford to lose $2,200 a month, pay a mortgage, and raise a family of five. He needed a new plan just to survive.

One morning he read the biblical story of Joseph, a Hebrew man who had been sold by his very own brothers into slavery. Joseph became the trusted administrator to the Egyptian governor Potiphar. Potiphar's wife tried to seduce Joseph, and when he refused her advances, she falsely accused him of trying to rape her. He was thrown in prison, where he interpreted the other prisoners' dreams. This God-inspired talent eventually resulted in Joseph's release from prison and an unexpected career move to become prime minister of Egypt, the second in authority to Pharaoh himself. Later, when Joseph was reunited with his brothers, he said, "You meant evil against me; but God meant it for good" (Gen. 50:20).

As Rusty read Joseph's story, he felt his spirits rise. If God could rescue a man rotting in prison, surely he could help an out-of-work timber worker who still had a little money in the bank. Rusty bowed his head and thanked God for his family and the many blessings in his life. He thanked God for the chance to look for a new job and asked God to direct and guide him to the right opportunity.

Rusty took out a yellow pad of paper and listed the challenges facing him:

1. Get my finances ready for living with little money.
2. Find a new job.

The first challenge meant he and his family would have to tighten their belts. Looking for new work proved to be challenging. His job search became an eight-hour-a-day job in itself. He gratefully accepted a position as assistant manager of a local pancake restaurant at lower wages than he was making at the mill. Rusty did everything possible to be an asset to the business. Three years later, the owner sold the business to Rusty on a long-term contract. Rusty had learned the same truth that Joseph discovered back in Egypt: no unexpected career move is unexpected by God—He has a plan.

When you keep a positive attitude, work hard, plan well, and let God direct your life, your greatest career crisis can become an unforeseen opportunity you never could have imagined.

The Tempting "Other Option"

Rusty did what many people dream about but few actually do. He went into business for himself. Starting your own business can be tempting, because it seems to offer what folks want out of life: independence, the freedom to call your own shots, being your own boss, and the potential to earn lots of money. Put these assumptions on hold for just a moment. Before you think about starting your own business, you should know three words: *proficiency, perseverance,* and *pride.* As you look at these three words, it should become clear to you in about three minutes how successful you would probably be in your own business.

Proficiency is doing something extremely well. It means you have a skill, a craft, a talent, a trade—either selling a product or providing a service—that people consider valuable and are willing to buy. Whether you're an expert at fixing radiators, building computers, or painting portraits, you must have something to sell. Recently I played golf with a businessman who owns dialysis centers for kidney patients. Though he's not proficient in the medical area of the business, he hires people who are. His talents are business management and promotion. By being proficient in these skills, he can provide a service that some people literally can't live without. Do you have a product or service that others are willing to buy?

Perseverance is the essential quality in business that keeps you from giving up amid the adversities and obstacles of daily work. All the great business people I've met have overcome significant problems. If you have a track record of giving up when the pressure is on, you'll never be a successful business owner. On the contrary, if you keep trying when the odds are stacked against you, you may be a candidate to be a successful business owner. Are you willing to persevere through difficulties and risk rejection, disappointment, and failure in order to succeed?

Pride in what you do is the third essential element for running your own business. Today, more than ever, people are conscious of the quality of the products and services they buy. How much or how little you care about your work shows in the final product. And the people who make it in business are the people committed to "doing it right." Do you have pride in what you do, and can you translate that commitment to excellence into goods or service that will keep people coming back?

Take Action! The Decision That's All Yours

Answering the question "What will I do for a living?" comes down to making smart, well-informed decisions. Let's review these choices. The few minutes you invest now could mean the difference in how much or how little you enjoy your work:

- What do your skills, talents, and interests along with your past work and nonwork successes tell you about how you've been designed?
- What "insignificant" decisions have become milestone choices that have ended up changing your work future for the better?
- When you consider all that you may still have to learn in your present job, what would it be like to stick it out and grow where you're planted?
- If you're facing an unexpected career decision, are you willing to consider that this present darkness is just a prelude to the dawn of a new opportunity that awaits you?
- Are you willing to know yourself better by completing the exercises in this book? Are you willing to expand your opportunities by enrolling in a class or seminar that would help you improve what you do best? Build your character by doing the hard jobs no one else will do.

The critical decision of what you'll do for a living rests on these choices. How soon and how well you make them may determine where you'll be and what you'll be doing years from now.

Taking the First Step

What should I start doing today to improve my job skills and insure my future earning capacity?

_____

_____

_____

How would improved discipline in my life make me a more valuable worker?

_____

_____

_____

4 How Will You Handle Money?

ON A RECENT PLANE TRIP TO TEXAS, a businessman from Washington found himself sitting next to a Catholic bishop from San Antonio. Somewhere between the complimentary soft drinks and the bag of peanuts, the two men began to talk. As they discussed the bishop's role in a large metropolitan city, the subject turned to two legislative bills that were up for vote in Washington State—one regarding abortion rights and the other regarding the right of physician-assisted suicide, or the "right to die."

The bishop said, "After years of working in the political arena, I've become convinced that all politics is motivated by money. I know of the big money being made by the abortion industry and why abortion is a political issue. But I haven't yet figured out who would benefit financially from the passage of the euthanasia bills."

This wise bishop did well to express a powerful truth: money is a mighty motivator. Because of its allure and its ability to secure earthly comfort, safety, and pleasure, money is involved in some of the stickiest problems you'll ever face. Though money can't buy friends or assure you of a happy home or a rewarding job, it can dictate your overall quality of life. And because money affects so many other decisions about what you can and can't afford—from food to clothing, from schooling to cars—how you handle money is one of the most critical decisions facing you every day for all of your life.

WHERE DOES MONEY COME FROM?

The question seems almost too simple to ask. Yet every person who finds himself or herself wanting "just a little bit more" always comes back to the basics. Money is produced by a combination of talent, hard work, and responsibility. To earn money, you need to invest the talent God has given you into meaningful and productive work. You can't sit on the sidelines of life and still receive the benefits that come from playing the game. By realizing that the source of all money is God, you can come to some startling conclusions about how biblical principles relate to money's true worth in your life.

My friend John Wordsworth grew up as a preacher's son. Since his father traveled a lot, John often looked after his four younger siblings and performed the tasks his dad would have done. John worked hard. Those early years of responsibility prepared him to be a sawmill worker and a fireman. He also had a good head for numbers and a gift for organization. John put these two talents to work as treasurer for his church. He enjoyed keeping books and developed a small, part-time bookkeeping service.

One of John's accounts was a floor covering company. Eventually he became the firm's business manager, and over the course of several years, he bought the company. He became one of the most successful hardwood floor dealers in the western United States. If he had not used his talents to serve his church, he may not have developed the bookkeeping skills that enabled him to eventually buy his own business.

Though John's business commitments increased, he remained active in his church. In fact, he often worked with other congregations by generously giving his valuable, practical business insights to church leaders who were buying land and buildings. John's growing real estate acumen helped many churches grow and prosper. This know-how helped him make wise real estate investments, which provided a source of income when he retired from his business.

John's business and personal life exemplified an Old Testament truth. As the Jewish people worked to build the temple, God improved their skills. The Bible points out that after the temple was finished, the newly enhanced skills of the people remained.

John's countless hours invested in service to his church were also multiplied back to him in the growth of his business skills. Without trying to prove God at His Word, he simply lived the truth found in Deut. 8:18: "You shall remember the LORD your God, for it is He who gives you power to get wealth."

Before we go any further, it's important to make one thing clear: *accumulating power or wealth is not the reason God wants you to serve Him.* Wealth and money are not automatic blessings that come from serving God. The Scriptures simply remind us that God is the source of all wealth. Therefore, anything we receive in the way of money is reason to give thanks to the Giver. It's like the feeling you get from opening a present—your appreciation naturally flows back to the giver.

John Wordsworth realized how much God had given to him, and his appreciation to the Giver flowed back to the Church in the form of hundreds of volunteer hours and thousands of dollars. In the process he discovered that behind his material wealth were priceless principles that could come only from God.

If you embrace this basic truth—*that God is the source of all money*—then you'll be able to appreciate the means by which that money reaches you.

> IF YOU EMBRACE THIS BASIC TRUTH—THAT GOD IS THE SOURCE OF ALL MONEY—THEN YOU'LL BE ABLE TO APPRECIATE THE MEANS BY WHICH THAT MONEY REACHES YOU.

Money may come to you from one or more sources. One way is through inheritance. Inherited money may become a real burden—without the skill and wisdom to manage it. I once knew a brother and sister who received a substantial inheritance. They invested in every get-rich scheme the town offered and soon lost all their parents' hard-earned assets.

You could choose to steal money. This acquisition method carries a high price tag, of course. You could be fined (now say "good-bye" to your money!), or if convicted and sentenced to jail, you could spend a lot of nights in the Gray Bar Hotel. Such a career move could also have a real impact on your future earning power.

By far the most common way to secure money through ethical, moral, and legal means is to earn it. This can happen through investments, but more commonly through work. Not only does this make sense in our free-market economy, but the work-for-pay principle is as old as the Bible itself: "Let him who stole steal no longer, but rather let him labor, working with his hands what is good, that he may have something to give him who has need" (Eph. 4:28).

Work is honorable. It's God's plan for our experience in asset management. Unfortunately, a lot of people talk and think about work as if it were a dirty word instead of a God-ordained institution. When you think about it, the first activity recorded in the Bible is work: "In the beginning God created the heavens and the earth" (Gen. 1:1). "And on the seventh day God ended His work which He had done, and He rested on the seventh day from all His work which He had done" (Gen. 2:2).

So you see, God not only believes in work, but He also practices it. In His work of the Creation, He set an example for us: six days of work and one day of rest. I've noticed that folks who follow this example are practicing good stewardship of their time and talents and seldom have major extended financial problems. Work is not only good for you—physically *and* emotionally—it also produces financial benefits that not only will take care of your family's needs, but will also give you a surplus so you can share with others. Now let's look at how *the way you work* influences *what you earn*.

1. **What you earn is determined by the scale of value of your work**. Every occupation, every type of work, has a scale of value: what people are willing to pay for the services or products rendered. This rule applies for doctors, plumbers, barbers, and bankers. It applies to *your* occupation. Everything you do professionally and personally comes with a scale of value. It's important for you to plan to grow within the scale of value that's accepted for the work you do. Don't get caught in the trap of comparing what you earn to what someone else earns. Different pay applies to different scales. Strive to be the most productive worker in your chosen work activity, and your wages will eventually reflect it.

2. **What you earn is determined by the demand for your work**. If you were to graduate from nursing school, you might find that nurses are in short supply, that there are more job opportunities than qualified people to fill them. In this kind of market, salaries will rise. *Whenever you have a skill that's hard to find or is in great demand, you will tend to make more money*. More people searching for fewer jobs means that companies can afford to hire the best-qualified people at a lower wage. People who understand this simple supply-and-demand equation and who want to increase their earning power develop skills that over time are in greater demand. Your personal responsibility is to keep your earning power at its peak by securing training to position you for work that people *need and are willing to pay for*.

3. **What you earn is determined by the quantity of your work**. I have known many folks like a friend of mine named Buzz. He did a good job at what he did, but he was so pokey he never accomplished much. He would shuffle papers, look at his work, go get a drink of water or a cup of coffee, sit down, and look at his work again. He put in a full day *at* work *without working* a full day. The work he did accomplish was always well done. Unfortunately, he never produced very much of it—and he was always complaining about how hard he worked. Buzz's low quantity of work kept him from receiving raises or promotions, and he had a hard time keeping a job.

I always felt that if Buzz had tackled his work with the enthusiasm he put into his hobbies, he would have been a great success. Unfortunately, he didn't, and his income suffered.

4. **What you earn is determined by the quality of your work**. True or false: People who do a high quality and a high quantity of work receive matching financial rewards. This is true. "But where I work, everyone gets paid the same, no matter what they do," some may say. In the short term this may be true, but life has a way of balancing the scales. If you stick with the principle that high-quality work gets rewarded, sooner or later the dollars will catch up with you.

Dave is a carpet installer who is a master craftsman. He is recognized as one of the best in his field. He not only does a high quality job, but he also is a quick and efficient worker. When he worked in a union shop, he was paid the same as his coworkers. But because of his skill and productivity, *he* was the worker his bosses preferred to have on the job, so he had more steady work. He has now started his own company and is in constant demand. He may now be the highest paid worker in his field. He is definitely at the high end of his work's scale of value.

5. **What you earn is determined by how you invest yourself in your work.** As I write this, I'm flying at 35,000 feet in a Boeing 757 headed from Seattle to Chicago. In front of me is a young man in his 20s. During the time we've been airborne, he has scoured several company reports, read two newsletters on business management, and reviewed a report on pending tax legislation. Now he's reading a textbook on small business management.

I would guess he's also taking an evening or weekend class in business—or he has a stake in his own firm. Either way, he has chosen to invest himself in his work. He may not see his "return on investment" for several years, but you can be sure of this: by the time he begins to reap the fruit of his labor, others who spent their time pursuing carefree or "careless" leisure, or who didn't invest their time wisely, will be saying, "Why does he get all the good breaks? I'm as talented as he is." What they don't realize is that *application,* not talent, creates opportunity.

What are you doing today to enhance the scale, the quality, the quantity, and the level of self-investment of your work? Are you making wise decisions to ensure your future earning potential?

WHERE SHOULD YOUR MONEY GO?

A basic rule of financial management is "Money will always follow a plan." Money, like a river's current, will flow in the course of its natural destination. In other words, if you don't have a plan for your money, it will flow to someone else who does have a plan for it. The supermarket has a plan for your money. So does your local auto dealer, carpet salesperson, and fast-food restaurant. If you don't have a plan for your money, you need one.

The stores are filled with magazines, tape series, guide books, and how-to plans that offer "the best way to handle your money." Look at all the "perfect plans," and one theme will become clear. Any sound money strategy is built on a combination of investing, saving, and giving away what you earn. Let me share with you some proven guidelines that can give you either a foundation to build on or a vantage point to review concerning your current money plan. With everything you earn

- Give away 10 percent
- Save 10 percent, and
- Learn to live on the remaining 80 percent

Let's look at each part:

1. Give away 10 percent of your income. On the surface, it seems that giving 10 percent "off the top" would be counterproductive to financial wisdom. But the opposite is true. The discipline of giving teaches you to be thankful. If you believe God is the source of everything you will ever earn, doesn't it make sense to acknowledge this fact by giving to His work a portion of what He's already given to you? When you develop the habit of giving, you're making an investment in a heavenly bank account that pays eternal dividends.

One day after I spoke in a meeting, a woman told me,

I know what you're talking about really works. God does reward our faithful giving. My husband and I were in the ministry for more than 20 years. We had always pastored small churches and never made a lot of money. Even though it was a struggle, we always paid to the church our tithe of 10 percent of our earnings, and we gave above that amount, whatever we could, for special offerings. Then my husband got sick with cancer. We were in the prime of our life and ministry. I didn't know what to do. I had never worked outside the home except for helping my husband pastor a church. I had always played the piano and done whatever I could to help him.

I tried to think of what I could do to get a job. The only thing that came to mind was our neighborhood supermarket—bagging groceries. I applied and got the job. It was a good job and paid more than I had dreamed of making. After I had been working for a while, another job opened for a grocery checker. When I took their test, I got the highest score ever achieved. I didn't know that all those years of playing the church piano were creating job skills. Today I'm the fastest checker in the store. The insurance policy from my job has paid for all of my husband's cancer treatments. We also owned a little house that we were able to fix up and sell at a nice profit. We have just purchased another one that we can do the same thing with. I found that God really does care for us!

Mal. 3:10 underlines this truth when God tells the Jews to "Bring the whole tithe into the storehouse, that there may be food in my house. Test me in this," says the LORD Almighty, and see if I will not throw open the floodgates of heaven and pour out so much blessing that you will not have room enough for it" (NIV). If you learn to be thankful and develop the "gift of giving," money will begin to loosen whatever control it may have had upon your life, and you will find your gifts multiplied beyond your dreams and expectations!

2. Save 10 percent of your income. There are three seasons in your life: your learning years, your earning years, and your yearning years.

Think about it. Most of us spend the first 20 years learning in school, the next 40 years earning a living, and the rest of our lives yearning for time to relax, reflect, and spend time with family. If we haven't been saving, we may also find ourselves yearning for money we don't have. A systematic savings plan provides you the money you may not be able to earn by the time your energy, health, and years are in short supply.

Don't let the excuse of "I don't earn enough" or "I don't know where to invest" keep you from making a regular trip to the bank. A systematic savings plan increases the financial discipline that can create added earning opportunities in your early years and therefore lessen the degree of yearning for income when your earning days are through.

3. Live on the remaining 80 percent of your income. In a credit card world where we flash our "plastic," it's easy to spend more than you really earn. Put this temptation on the shelf and ask yourself, "What would it look like for me [us] to live on 80 percent of what we make?"

I would guess that you will need to set spending priorities. If you decide in advance where and how much you'll spend, living on 80 percent (or the "10-10-80" plan, as I call it) suddenly becomes a realistic goal. You'll resist buying depreciating assets like cars, furniture, and appliances on credit. Instead of spending money you don't have, you can develop a "save-to-spend" account. This is not your savings account, but a deferred spending fund that rewards your decision to defer a certain amount of funds to pay cash for a big-ticket item.

People who live on 80 percent find they can live a good-quality yet modest lifestyle. They don't have to "keep up with the Joneses." They're not constantly fighting to get out of debt, because money's grip has now been loosened—as God intended.

What Will Your Money Do?

Isn't it interesting how often we think about how money can benefit us and how rarely we consider what it could do for someone else? Have you ever considered how a disciplined savings plan could give you a financial surplus to help you support deserving people and projects? With your money

- **You can be a giving leader by helping worthwhile programs that lack needed funds**. I'm sure you can think of several causes you believe in. Behind each program is a real need that can benefit from your generosity. Few joys compare with being able to support worthy organizations you believe in.

- **You can be the booster of a person who dreams of going to college, needs costly medical attention, or feels called to serve in missions**. Someone in your neighborhood, church, company, or school is facing a financial need that you may be able to meet. By helping this person, you affirm a set of values and open the door to building a relationship with that person who is doing something you believe in. You can make a big difference in someone else's life by providing a little financial help.

TAKE ACTION! RESULTS THAT MONEY CAN'T BUY

When you look at the your checkbook register, your outstanding bills, the amount you've saved, the amount you've spent, the amount you've given to others—are you handling money, or is money handling you? Is your money following your plan or someone else's?

Before the alarm clock rings on Monday morning, invest an hour in making the following decisions:

- **Determine who and what have shaped your view about money.** Match this approach against the biblical wisdom in this chapter, and then decide on the principles that will guide your day-to-day choices about money.

- **Look at the scale of value, quantity, quality, market demand, and degree of self-investment in your work**. Then ask, "Can any of these things be enhanced to increase my earning potential?"

- **Ask, "Is there any reason I can't live by the '10-10-80' plan?"** How do these reasons stack up against the principles you listed above?

- **Commit now to how you will handle your next paycheck**. Decide now where the money will go.

When you've put down your pencil or look up from the calculator, I trust you'll have a better handle on your money than you did before. You may not believe it, but the decision you've already begun to make will in some way affect your bottom line. Whether you eventually end up with more money is not as important as what you do with the money—and what the money does to you.

Taking the First Step

What three habits will I start today that will help me enhance my financial future?

1. _____

2. _____

3. _____

5 How Will You Deal with Temptation?

HAVE YOU EVER DREAMED you were being chased by a monster? At first you were probably startled. The shock turned to fear. The fear turned to panic. Then the panic simply overwhelmed you. At first you tried to run. But no matter how hard you pumped your arms and legs, the monster kept getting bigger and closer. Just when you thought you gained a step, it took one giant step and moved in front of you!

What a terrible feeling! When you tried to hide, the monster was already there, waiting and lurking. When you thought you had ditched the beast for good, there it was again, never letting go, never giving up on the chance to devour you.

This is more than an imaginary dream. What I've just described is another kind of animal that roams through our lives, an unseen monster called temptation. Of all the critical decisions you will make in life, none may help you avoid more painful and damaging consequences than your decision to resist temptation. I don't mean just sexual temptation, but *any* temptation—any fascination, enticement, or lure that would rob you of the best God has for you and those you love.

Temptation has many faces, some so subtle and hidden that this monster could be breathing down your neck and you might not even know it.

Why is the threat of temptation so potentially destructive?

How can you avoid the consequences of temptation so that even when the monster seems to gain ground, you don't have to be its victim?

TEMPTATION'S DESTRUCTIVE NATURE

What *is* temptation? When you peel off its fancy wrapper that promises pleasure and gain, what's really at the core of temptation? The third chapter of Genesis tells us in a familiar yet timeless story.

It was a beautiful day in Eden. Eve was walking on a carpet of soft grass, her bare feet gently caressed by the morning dew. As she gathered fruit from the many trees, she glanced at the tree of the knowledge of good and evil. She knew God had forbidden her to eat of its fruit. But she thought it might not hurt to look. She walked closer. In the tree was a beautiful creature. Its hypnotic green eyes transfixed Eve in a seductive stare.

Gradually, the serpent convinced Eve to taste the fruit of the tree, and she succumbed. With hungry curiosity she took the fruit and tasted for herself—giving in to temptation. What seemed like a simple, harmless decision quickly ate into her very being.

The consequence of Eve's and Adam's decision to eat—their choice to follow the serpent rather than follow God—produced fateful consequences: "And the LORD God said, 'The man has now become like one of us, knowing good and evil. He must not be allowed to reach out his hand and take also from the tree of life and eat, and live forever" (Gen. 3:22, NIV).

- The destructive core of temptation is saying "yes" to self and "no" to God.

- The ultimate, destructive consequence of giving into temptation is death.

- Though the allure may seem sweet, rewarding, and irresistible, temptation's false promise, from Eden's day to ours, always leads to decay and demise.

Choose to follow temptation, and you'll experience the full depth of its shallow promise:

Yielding to temptation destroys your self-confidence and erodes your self-image.

- It attacks your creativity and dulls your giftedness.

- Temptation's "fruit" is a shrinking sense of potential.
- Temptation's backwash leaves you feeling dirty inside.
- Temptation's residue pollutes a clear conscience and upright character.
- Temptation's footprint makes you want to cover your own tracks.

This can take away valuable time and energy you'll never get back, time you could invest in the people and things you really care about—your friendships, your marriage, your job, your relationship with God.

Many people have succumbed to the temptation of fast money and have paid a bitter price for it. Take the case of Simon. He was a respected small business owner. He was an active church member, good father, and well-liked guy. Then his business began to experience difficult times, and his financial problems mounted. An unexpected opportunity to make some fast, big money arose. He had only to take a couple of guys back and forth to Canada on the weekends in his boat. He agreed. They were eventually arrested for smuggling drugs, and he spent the next few years in jail.

Mary had what many women dream about: a good husband, two lovely children, a nice home, and good friends. Then a new family moved in next door. The man worked swing shift, and his wife worked days. What started out as a friendly conversation about gardening escalated into an affair that culminated in two broken homes and many broken hearts. Mary didn't plan on things developing like that. She was blinded by temptation.

TEMPTATION'S DESTRUCTIVE THREAT

Even though we've never met, I know you've been tempted in some way by your own desires, attitudes, or friends in the last week. How do I know? Because you're human. Your human nature, like *my* human nature, seeks security, pleasure, and comfort. Because our need for these things is so basic, so inbred, and so strong, we may say "yes" to temptation even when we know our unwise choice won't really satisfy our true need.

Why is temptation so potentially destructive? While you're being tempted, your only goal is to satisfy one person—*you*. When you're tempted to not report your true income to the government, the only person you're looking out for is *you*. When you're tempted to start an illicit relationship, the only person you really want to satisfy is *you*. When you're tempted to tell others how you were wronged by someone else, the only person whose reputation you care about is *yours*.

Temptation always promises more than it can deliver. More than that, the "promise" of temptation is a false claim that leaves us unfulfilled, unsatisfied, less content, and more frustrated than before. Temptation is a cheap hamburger masquerading as sirloin steak, a sour ball disguised as sweet chocolate fudge. The outside is wonderfully irresistible, the inside woefully disappointing.

The danger of temptation is that you can be lured into a situation that opposes what you believe. And by the time you wake up to the truth, your nightmare-of-a-monster-you-can't-escape has become reality.

Today you and I live in the fallen shadow of Adam and Eve's selfish decision. When you were born, you entered a world ripe with temptation. You didn't have a choice. Temptation isn't a piece of fiction you can pick up or put down at will—it's a real fact that's been written into the pages of our lives. You and I will have to deal with temptation for the rest of our lives. Before you can know how to effectively deal with temptation, we need to look at how temptation comes to us. What does the serpent look like in our day?

Three Ways We're Tempted

I've seen temptation take three very basic forms. The unspectacular, everyday appearance of this monster may surprise you.

1. Desires. Our natural, human hunger for pleasure can be a temptation. The desire for food can lead to a great variety of tastes (and calories!). If unchecked, this desire can make its unhealthful impact in the form of added weight, high blood pressure, and high cholesterol. All other natural physical desires, when used improperly, have the same, and even more serious, potential for disastrous side effects.

2. Attitudes. What does our thinking have to do with temptation? Negative attitudes create thoughts and actions that harm our well-being. When was the last time you felt wronged by another person? What did you do with those feelings? If you held onto them, your feelings of injustice may have bubbled into anger, resentment, bitterness, and even hatred. With each new emotion you had the opportunity to deal with the situation or be tempted to hold onto the particular feeling. Which choice did you make? Even if you decided to resolve the matter, can you appreciate now the fact that unchecked attitudes are a source of temptation?

3. Friends. Imagine the people you know and trust the most tempting you! It happens. Why? Because you and I want to be liked. We want to feel accepted. We want to know our opinions and beliefs matter to others. As a result, we're tempted to do or say something to satisfy our "need to belong," even if that means compromising a cherished personal relationship or belief.

As a young man I decided I would not drink alcoholic beverages. Many times friends and people I've wanted to impress have offered me alcohol. The simple act of saying "No thank you" has often required personal courage for someone with a strong need to be liked and accepted.

It *is* possible to resist temptation. It *is* possible to go your own way, to live up to a higher standard and not live down to laziness and uncaring. Even though Adam and Eve sampled the forbidden fruit, and even though we have been eating rotten fruit ever since, it *is* possible to get the upper hand on temptation. The key lies not in knowing how to respond but in knowing *how to anticipate and prepare yourself* for that moment when you will be unexpectedly tempted. By knowing how to respond, having made a commitment to deny temptation before it happens, temptation can actually become a valuable stepping stone to building integrity, patience, and conviction into your character.

By saying "No!" to temptation's whisper, you can discover a new sense of self-confidence. You can experience true personal freedom. These positive feelings and emotions can lead to a whole new sense of achievement and personal fulfillment. The biggest payoff, however, is the inner peace that comes from overcoming temptation, from doing without something (or someone) that could harm you deeply. You quickly learn that you really haven't "done without" anything—but have gained something far greater through your denial of temptation's empty promises.

How do you get an upper hand on temptation? By planning ahead and living proven principles.

If you were going into battle, you would want to learn as much about your enemy as possible. You would study your opponent's behavior and try to understand when and where he or she would be likely to attack. If you wanted to avoid being captured, enslaved or defeated—*in other words, if you wanted to live*—you would learn all about your opponent's weapons and strategies.

The same is true as you battle with temptation. A wise person will make some firm decisions on how to thwart temptation in advance.

With a planned strategy, you can anticipate temptation before it occurs and win life's battles in your weak and vulnerable areas. With a planned strategy based on God's wisdom and strength—so much greater than human thinking and human effort—you can turn your temptations into stepping stones of achievement. If you create a plan using the practical steps below, make a commitment and stick to it. Then you have effectively won most of the battle before it begins.

1. Find encouragement and strength in the company of others.

The first step is to know that you're not alone. Everyone

is tempted every day. You and I cannot escape temptation. The Bible says, "No temptation has seized you except what is common to man" (1 Cor. 10:13, NIV).

You and I live in a world in which the resident serpent has had millennia to practice. He knows our weaknesses: to be liked by others, to bend the truth, not to want to part with our money, to satisfy our desires. Let's face it: the serpent knows us better than we know ourselves. The snakelike maven of temptation warms up to us as a friend but seeks our destruction.

Because everyone you know has been tempted, you can look for avenues of appropriate sharing. You can pray for people who face common struggles, and in your fellowship you can know you are not alone. You can find the encouragement and strength that comes when Christians meet and pray for each other.

Finding others you can tell about your temptations is another way of saying, "I can't make it on my own." No one can overcome temptation without help. If Eve had told Adam she was being tempted, together they may have been strong enough to resist the serpent. Today your encouragement, your "help," may be closer than you think. You may have been born into a family who genuinely knows how to support you. If so, resist the temptation to make it on your own. (Yes, even this is a temptation.) Receive their love and their willingness to listen and care.

Perhaps you were born into a family who has tempted you to get angry, give up, and retreat. Maybe you have never had the support you wanted. Families, like all groups, *can* and *do* change. You and members of your family can show a change of heart. The temptation to remain separate and "safely" away from each other may give way to healthy, growing relationships. Meanwhile, you may want to find a support group for the encouragement you need. Many wonderful people give their lives to help others improve. A wholesome, caring group of friends from your church or job may give you the "space and place" of assurance and community you need to survive and win battles over temptation.

For several months I met regularly with a good friend named Claude Terry. We held each other accountable for our actions. Among the questions we asked each other when we met was "How have you been tempted, and how did you respond?" Your spouse, your pastor, your friends, and your colleagues are all people you could ask to hold you accountable.

A few years ago my nephew Dan Tyner approached me to be his mentor. At that time he was 22 years old. I felt a great deal of freedom to offer him suggestions on how to develop as a person, to ask him some tough questions, and to "hold his feet to the fire." Dan has grown a great deal over the years.

Bill McCartney, former football coach for the University of Colorado, wanted to help build character in men and founded Promise Keepers. From the first group of 70 men who met in 1990, the ministry has mushroomed into an international men's movement of multiplied thousands. Many men from my church in Seattle have attended Promise Keepers gatherings of worship, prayer, and mutual support. The results for these men have been spectacular. One reason, I believe, is that Promise Keepers is founded on the principle of accountability, of encouraging men to keep their promises to God, their family, and friends.

I've seen the life-changing results that come from men holding other men accountable for their actions. One individual who travels shared his temptation to watch adult movies in his hotel room. He asked a member of this men's accountability group to call the hotels at which he will stay and have the cable television disconnected in his room before he arrives.

A person's confessed weakness can be a powerful asset. By admitting what you're unable or unwilling to do on your own, you can call on friends.

2. Make God your greatest resource.

The second thing, and actually the most important thing, you can do to reduce the threat of succumbing to temptation is to look to God. One thing I like best about the Bible is that it is clear and absolute. The Ten Commandments are not titled "The Ten Hints for Successful Living." They are rules of behavior. Either you're in harmony with them, or you're not.

When it comes to dealing effectively with temptation, God's directives can be translated into three words:

1. Avoid. Translation: don't mess with things you know may get you in trouble. A man I know is addicted to gambling and has lost thousands of dollars. His future economic security depends to a great extent on his ability to avoid gambling. Because he knows his areas of temptation, he doesn't subscribe to horse racing news. He avoids exposure to areas where he knows he is weak against the strong attack of temptation.

2. Resist. Victory in the temptation war is usually achieved by winning small battles. Resist the small temptation of not depositing the required amount at a "self-pay" parking lot, and you're more likely to resist the temptation of not reporting your true income to your government. The small, seemingly "unimportant" decisions help us build integrity and strengthen our weapons against temptation—one decision at a time.

I knew a woman named Kathy who once received $5 too much in change after paying for her groceries. *What luck!* she thought. *This will help me stretch my grocery budget.* Kathy didn't realize the grocery store needed the $5 as much as she did. And she almost didn't grasp the real ethical issue: as she held the $5, she thought, *If I keep this money, I'm stealing.*

What would you do if you were in Kathy's shoes?

She could keep the money. Or she could give back what was not rightly hers. Had Kathy kept the money, what do you think she would have been tempted to do the next time she faced a similar temptation? That day Kathy did the right thing —she returned the money. "You gave me too much," she said with a smile to the clerk. In this small decision, she laid another stone in the lifetime process of building character and prepared herself to resist future enticements.

3. Flee. Sometimes, despite our best efforts, our plans to

avoid temptation fail. At these times the wise thing to do is
flee.

I remember the story of a salesman, Ken, whose company
sent him to a trade show in Dallas. The display booth next to
Ken's was occupied by a cute saleswoman with a charming ac-
cent. Ken enjoyed her company. Whenever business slowed,
they talked. At the end of the second day, as they were closing
their booths, the woman told Ken she was going to the hotel
bar to have a drink and relax. The invitation was obvious. Ken
faced a decision: he could go to his hotel room, or he could
spend the evening with this attractive woman. Ken thanked
her for the invitation and said he had to finish some paper-
work, starting "right away." Ken knew when to flee.

TAKE ACTION! UNSEEN STRENGTH IS AVAILABLE NOW

It's tempting to think that conquering temptation is a
matter of simply following several suggestions. The real power
to overcome temptation, however, lies outside of you—with
God. Because God is immensely personal, loving, and practical, He invites us to take simple, practical steps that allow us
to draw upon His power.

- **Commit Bible principles and verses to memory**. The
  psalmist said, "Your word I have hidden in my heart,
  That I might not sin against You!" (Ps. 119:11). The
  more you internalize the principles in the Bible, the
  more likely it is that you'll live according to God's Word.

- **Build a base of prayer support**. Prayer is powerful.
  You can build a prayer support base by participating in
  prayer groups, developing relationships with people
  who pray, and praying regularly yourself. When Jesus'
  disciples asked Him to teach them to pray, He taught
  them the Lord's Prayer. Part of the prayer is "And lead
  us not into temptation, but deliver us from the evil one"
  (Matt. 6:13, NIV). You can prepare for temptation
  through a disciplined and joyous prayer life.

- **Practice forgiving others—and yourself**. Being tempted is part of being human. Human beings fail. One of
  life's greatest joys and hopes, however, is knowing that
  God forgives us when we go astray. This doesn't mean
  we should do what we know is wrong so we can experience the love and acceptance of a forgiving God. It
  means that the more you experience God's forgiveness,
  the more you're able to forgive yourself as well as others.

God holds out a permanent safety net to catch us when
we fall. Every time we lose to temptation and skip off the
high-wire of life, we're "caught" by His love, and it's a little
easier to forgive.

Without depending on God, you and I are helpless
against temptation. Right now the temptation monster in your
life may look overwhelming. Call on God, however, and you'll
begin to see temptation for what it really is—less of a monster
and more of a toothless nuisance you can gladly overcome.

TAKING THE FIRST STEP

What temptation do I face most often?

_____

_____

What can I do to deal with this temptation more effectively?

_____

_____

6 How Will You Respond to Adversity?

July 22, 1984, started as a beautiful day, with the pale blue Seattle sky broken only by an occasional wispy cloud. I was flying to San Diego, where I expected an even warmer reception.

The flight was pleasant, and I was delighted to find my rental car had been upgraded from a compact to a new Lincoln. I chuckled as I told myself, *Sometimes you can't control your own good fortune.*

That afternoon I drove to Anaheim, where I planned to spend the night in a nice hotel, speak to a group of sales executives the next morning, and then drive back to San Diego for two more speaking dates before flying home.

That night I learned the Seattle Mariners were playing a baseball game against the California Angels. Since the stadium was just a few minutes away, I couldn't say no. After a few innings, my home team fell behind seven to nothing. Since I knew there was no chance of getting in the lineup and helping the team make a comeback, I decided to leave. I had plenty to do in my room to prepare for the next day's speech.

I pulled into the hotel parking lot. As I stepped out of the car, another vehicle pulled up behind me, and three men jumped out. One had a shotgun. He came around the front of my car and pointed the barrel right at me—with only a few feet between the trigger and my head. Suddenly, my world became a nightmare in slow motion. Disbelief and panic rushed through me. *Is this really happening?* I thought.

In that moment of shock, sweat, and fear, I turned my back on the gun and ran. I didn't get far before the shotgun went off. It sounded like a cannon and felt like a sledgehammer on my back. I stumbled. Somehow I managed to stay on my feet and keep running. At that instant, all the motivational seminars I had ever attended seemed distant. But for some reason, at that particular point in my life, I became extremely goal-oriented. I could think only of making it to the hotel lobby. And I did, grabbing the handle of the front door, fighting to breathe and get the words out of my mouth—"I've been shot! Call the police!"

The desk clerk stared as I slumped to the floor. She didn't pick up the phone. My back felt seared. As I lay there, with my life's blood soaking the carpet, I could see people looking at me, but no one seemed willing to get close to me. Finally a good Samaritan walked to where I was lying. He said, "He *has* been shot."

Suddenly everyone sprang into action. Within minutes the police and medics were on the scene.

"He's been wasted," one medic said. I was rolled onto a stretcher. Then, looking at strange faces I slid, into the back of an ambulance.

When we arrived at the emergency room, the ambulance doors opened, and in seconds I ended up in a brightly lit examining room.

"Does he speak English?" someone yelled. Two people with clipboards appeared. They needed my social security number and a financial statement. Even in the best circumstances, I've had a hard time filling out forms. However, I had never held a pen while lying on my back, attached to life support systems. I tried to answer the questions.

Then more commotion. A police officer wanted me to tell him what happened. A police photographer asked to have me rolled over while he took some pictures. I was glad to be alive. But the worst was yet to come.

The emergency room team soon patched me up, with tubes and needles sticking out of and into my body. Next it was time for x-rays. Then I was wheeled back into the emergency room, where a nurse appeared with a bottle. He asked me to give him a urine specimen. I didn't know whether to laugh or cry. Here I was, flat on my back, with tubes attached to all parts of my body, and he wanted me to fill a bottle. I wanted to cooperate, but the challenge seemed greater than my ability.

When the nurse left, I had no luck. A few minutes passed, and the nurse was back to check on my progress. When he saw I was not cooperating, he yelled, "We need a sample! If you can't produce one, we'll have to take one and that'll hurt a lot!"

At that moment the one thing I didn't need was more pain. For the next 30 minutes the nurse checked on me. Finally he said, "You have five more minutes before we take a sample."

By this time, I was distressed. "Dear God," I prayed, "please help me do what I cannot." Immediately my bladder released. It was wonderful to be reminded that in my hour of crisis and adversity, the Lord was with me. Through the entire experience, from the moment the medics arrived to my departure from the hospital three days later, I felt peace in my heart. I knew God was in charge of my life and that whatever He wanted to do with me was OK. That night I was on the phone with my wife, Darlys, reassuring her that everything would be all right. And it was.

The next morning I read in the newspaper that I had been shot during a robbery attempt by three men who had held up three hotels that evening. I just happened to be in the parking lot at the wrong time.

That evening changed my life as I faced the fact that adversity is part of life. I could have recalled that evening in Anaheim as merely a tragic scene, a bad memory, a reason to rail against society's ills as a victim.

But I've not looked at it that way. Instead, that unplanned date with armed rage has become a valuable illustration of a truth none of us really wants to face.

In our world, adversity is an inevitable fact that will cause us to ask one of two questions: "Why me?" or "How will I deal with adversity?"

The first question will lead you to play the role of the

helpless victim. However, the second question can deepen your character, strengthen your endurance, and help you face future hardships with greater confidence.

Here are three reasons why you can't afford not to ask yourself, "How will I deal with adversity?"

1. You can expect adversities. No matter who you are or what you're doing in life, sooner or later, you will face challenges and hardships and adversities. As Job 5:17 says, "Man is born to trouble as surely as sparks fly upward" (NIV). Adversity may strike in a parking lot in southern California, in an airplane, or in your kitchen.

- You may go in for a routine physical checkup and hear the doctor say, "The tests turned up something new since your last visit. I'm afraid you have cancer."

- You may be trying to direct a big business deal. Gradually, decisions beyond your control take over. The deal unravels, and you lose most of your money—money you were counting on to fund your retirement.

- Some Friday afternoon as you're preparing to leave work, you learn you've been terminated. Suddenly the thought of raising two children without any regular income seems impossible.

- You may come home one day to find a note on the table. Your spouse wants a divorce.

- You may get a phone call from your newly married daughter saying she's been diagnosed with leukemia.

These seem like extreme cases, unless a similar instance has already happened to you, a family member, or a friend. These situations have all happened to close friends of mine.

Adversity can threaten a cherished relationship, a job, the core of your self-image, or your very life. I consider myself an eternal optimist. Whenever I face a risky situation, I usually see the glass as half full rather than half empty. Yet I also know that, like Job, I'm human. And being human means living in a world filled with disappointments and sorrows, unfulfilled promises and shattered hopes.

Getting shot was certainly one of the scariest adversities

I've ever faced; yet over the years I've experienced other serious hardships:

- Business deals that went sour
- The pain of friends who betrayed my confidence
- The loss of my father when I was 17 years old
- The struggle to survive and achieve on my own
- The results of poor decisions and faulty planning.

Based on my friends' experiences and my own, I've come to expect adversities in life. They may not be life-and-death struggles that "happen to someone else." Your next bout of adversity may be a rainy, four-mile walk to the nearest gas station because your car has broken down. Adversity may take the form of a wrestling match of wills with your teenager, or hurt feelings that linger between you and a friend. The degree of adversity may differ—yet adversity is not a question of "if" but "when."

The sooner you choose to expect adversity, the more time you'll have to plan for your response to hardship. By anticipating adversity, you can find unexpected worth in the midst of inevitable agonies.

2. You can find opportunity in adversities. Even though it's sometimes hard to know where to look, good can come out of any experience in your life. After all, even a broken clock is right twice a day!

The night I was in the hospital feeling the sting of a shotgun blast, I thought, "What good can come from being shot?"

Good things? Yes, good things came from being sprayed by a hundred lead pellets that could have killed me. Over the coming weeks, I confirmed the "good" thoughts:

Because of the adversity of being shot, I did not swing as hard when I played golf, and by swinging with less effort I hit the ball straighter.

Because of the adversity of being shot, I now had a great attention-getting story as part of my speeches to groups.

Because of the adversity of being shot, I could see how much physical, mental, and emotional stamina I had.

Because of the adversity of being shot, I discovered positive things about myself and life that I never would have experienced otherwise.

The key to reveling in a better golf swing and finding new levels of personal endurance was *choosing to accept* my circumstances. I decided I would not blame anyone for my tragedy. If I had blamed myself for going to the ball game, I could have shouldered a lot of damaging guilt. If I had blamed the man who shot me, I would have stirred anger, bitterness, and resentfulness. I needed to accept the fact that this unfortunate circumstance happened and then keep moving ahead with my life.

Here's the thing I learned: *accepting adversity opens the door to positive, unforeseen opportunities.* Don't get me wrong. I don't mean to paper over genuine loss with a cheap veneer of imitation joy. Real opportunity comes when you look at adversity head on, admit the real pain, and then ask God to help you see the ashes of your loss as the charcoal that can rekindle a new fire, a new start at life.

3. You can learn from your adversities. People who expect adversity are ready to face hardship when it comes. Adversity doesn't take them off guard; rather, it takes them to a deeper level of growth. That's what happened to Don James. In 1988 he took his University of Washington football team to the Sun Bowl to face the University of Alabama. We read the headlines of the Crimson tide's one-sided victory over the Huskies that day. What those headlines don't tell us is the story of how Washington's head coach grew from the adversity of that day.

James realized that his team had lost because Alabama had faster and quicker players. For years he had recruited college football players for their strength and size on the belief that bigger was better.

After the Alabama loss, that argument held little weight. James began recruiting players for their speed too. The Huskies became faster—and better. In 1991 they compiled an undefeated record and won a share of the National Championship. Not only did James accept the adversity from losing, but he also found that hardship gives birth to opportunity—an opportunity to let his team's weakness be the catalyst to become a winner.

Because my father died at an early age, I developed a hunger for the advice of older "father figures." This has produced a great source of diversified knowledge and information that I might have missed had I not responded positively to being without a father.

TAKE ACTION! HOW TO MAKE ADVERSITY YOUR ALLY TODAY

Before this week is over, perhaps before the end of this day, you could find yourself staring at real adversity. You will either grope frantically for someone or something you think will give you comfort and security, or you will respond to adversity with confidence and hope. Which way will you choose?

Consider the focus in your life. Job had everything. The Bible says he was "blameless and upright, and one who feared God and shunned evil" (Job 1:1). He had so many possessions he was considered "the greatest of all the people of the East" (Job 1:3). Suddenly, though, Job was destitute. He lost all he had—his family, possessions, everything! Job struggled at first. Finally, though, he accepted his situation and began to pray for his friends who had tried to "spiritualize" his condition. The Bible says God then restored him and doubled what he had before.

Job faced one of the greatest hazards of adversity: becoming absorbed in oneself and forgetting about others' needs.

Recently I visited a young woman who was hospitalized with a serious illness. I noticed that even though she was sick, she cheered up her family and friends, joking and laughing and keeping people from dwelling on the fact that she was ill. I wasn't surprised to learn that she eventually recovered. In fact, I'm sure the rooms of her home still ring with laughter.

When you focus on others instead of yourself or your adversity, you see where the power of love comes from—God. When adversity comes, what would it look like for you to focus on others and God instead of yourself? You say you're not so sure what you would do? You might be surprised at what can happen when you *choose* to look beyond the immediate struggle. You may be surprised to find some people have needs as great, if not greater, than your own. In focusing on others, you may discover a loving God who focuses on others, too, and wants to give—if you'll only ask.

Consider the circumstances within your control. When adversity strikes, list all of the circumstances in your control that contributed to your adversity. Then ask, "What could I change in the future that would produce more positive circumstances?" After you've looked at your responses, ask, "Is it worth it to make these changes?" If so, it may be time for you to take action.

Give thanks in adversities. While some circumstances seem impossible, many times the bumps we experience on the road of life actually guide and shape us. Too often we concentrate on specific events and fail to look at the way a negative can produce a positive.

When Venita Van Caspel's husband was killed in an airplane crash, she was unprepared to manage the money she received in the insurance settlement. Before she made any financial decisions, however, she took a class in investments. She found she liked studying money management. To learn more about the field, she took a secretarial job in a securities company. Eventually she built her own investment firm and became one of the nation's best-selling authors on personal investments, with her books on personal financial management used as textbooks around the world.

What would have happened if Venita had become bitter over her husband's death? By her actions, she chose to start from where she was and keep on living. She chose to use the resources God had given her. Instead of being terrified of the financial decisions, Venita decided, "There's so much I have to learn about money." This attitude of humility, combined with a desire to help others, has helped thousands enjoy a richer life.

What would happen if you decided to be thankful for your adversities as well as your blessings? Rom. 8:28 says,

"We know that all things work together for good to those who love God, to those who are the called according to his purpose." Anything that happens in your life, including adversity, can produce good.

Calvin Jones was an All-American defensive back at the University of Washington in the late 1960s. Being one of the 22 best college football players in the country, Calvin looked forward to playing in the National Football League. In fact, on the day of the pro draft, he thought he would be selected in one of the first three rounds. But he wasn't. On the second day of the draft he received a phone call and heard, "Congratulations! You've been drafted by the Denver Broncos." Just 5'9" tall and 165 pounds, Calvin thought his "low" draft pick meant that National Football League scouts believed he was too short, too small to play pro football.

Blessed with natural talent and firmly committed to be the best player he could, he did everything possible to prepare himself for the Broncos' training camp. He ran until he was so fatigued he would stop and throw up. Then he ran some more. He lifted weights with a new dedication. On the day he left for training camp, Calvin stopped to see his father, who was a pastor in San Francisco. His dad asked him what he felt his chances were to make the team. Calvin said, "Dad, I'm such a low draft choice I don't think they really plan on me making it. I've worked hard to get in shape. I know the Bible says all things work together for good to them who love the Lord and are called according to his purpose. That's me, Dad, and whatever God has in mind for me is OK, even if it doesn't include professional football."

That year Calvin Jones was a starting defensive back for the Broncos, one of the best defensive teams in professional football. He played four more years until an injury cut short his pro career. One day he told me, "Ralph, I've found all things work together for good if you love the Lord. If I had been a high draft choice, I might not have worked as hard to get in shape. I might not have even made the team."

Calvin said "thanks" to the adversity of being small by trying his best to make the team. How he dealt with adversity changed his life beyond football. After his career with the Broncos, he went into the ministry and today helps inner-city youth find meaning for their lives. His football credentials have been a great asset to him in his lifework.

Do we always give thanks? You may ask, "Ralph, are you thankful you were shot?" I can honestly tell you, "Yes, I am." Because of that experience, I rethought my priorities in life and made some decisions that have produced blessings I'm sure I would otherwise have never known.

I have learned to know God's peace in life's most anxious moments. When I was wounded and felt my blood oozing into the hotel carpet, I knew that God was with me and that whatever happened would be all right. I decided, as a result of my experience, that it paid big dividends in life's dark moments to have spent some time developing a personal relationship with God when everything seemed to be going well.

I also decided that it's a good idea to keep your personal relationships in good condition so that when you're at the point of leaving this world, you won't have regrets. As I thought about dying, I thought of some people to whom I needed to apologize. I hope the next time I'm in that situation, I won't have any regrets or unfinished business.

When bad things happen in your life, God can help you turn adversity into victory. If I really believe God is in control of my life—if I believe He's sovereign and controls all things—then I know anything that happens in my life has the potential to produce ultimate good.

What do *you* believe about adversity—and how will *you* respond to "impossible" challenges?

TAKING THE FIRST STEP

When have I personally experienced adversity that turned into a blessing?

What practical steps can I take this week to prepare for possible adversity in the future?

_____

_____

_____

7 WHAT WILL YOU DO WHEN YOUR DECISIONS FAIL?

SOMETIMES LIFE WEARS A DISGUISE, and what we see isn't the way things really are. Sometimes, seeing the difference between appearance and reality can bring joy. Sometimes a glimpse of the truth can change your life.

It happened to me one Sunday morning as I was leaving church. I looked up and saw a long-time family friend.

"How are you?" I asked.

"Just great," she said. It was a common response with an uncommon ring. Something was different. Maybe it was her confident tone of voice. Maybe it was the warm, clear look in her eye or the firm way she shook my hand. Maybe it was all these things that told me, "Rebecca really means what she says. She really does feel great."

And here's why this surprised me. Only nine weeks earlier, Rebecca's husband had left her for another woman. Yet on this morning her face, her manner radiated confidence. Despite what had happened, she was genuinely at peace. How on earth could this be? Rebecca's happiness didn't rest on someone else's tragic decision. True, she loved her husband. True, she was hurt deeply. Yet Rebecca had discovered that even though decisions fail, even though people fail, *she could still decide how she would respond to her circumstances.* In this woman I saw a very courageous person standing confidently in spite of a very real predicament.

Sooner or later even your best decisions are not going to work out.

Though you're not a spectator and you have participated in the decision at some level, you don't really have much control over the carnage. The hard truth is that failed decisions hurt. A failed decision means you stand to lose something cherished. You may lose your dignity. You may lose money. You may lose your sense of self. You may lose the desire to go on.

Failed decisions are a "given" in life—and so is your response to those decisions. The real question you need to grapple with is this: *What will you do when your decisions fail?*

How you respond to this question will determine if you will be able to get up when you're knocked down and if you'll decide to keep going and find renewed purpose, direction, and strength—or settle for far less than all that God wants to give you.

Mistakes are unavoidable. However, you can minimize the potential damage caused by decisions that go sour—even decisions beyond your control.

THREE WAYS WE EXPERIENCE FAILED DECISIONS

1. The impact of other people's decisions. The summer between my fourth and fifth grades was filled with fishing trips and berry picking—and sadness. One August morning two strangers wearing formal coats and official smiles knocked at our front door. From that day on my life was never the same-all because of someone else's decisions made long, long ago.

At an early age, my father developed chronic asthma. Imagine your lungs being no bigger than a school lunch bag. Imagine taking a few breaths, then gasping for more air and finding none. This is how my dad lived. Fighting to breathe became a daily battle. In the early 1950s the battle became a war. Across the country, including in the quiet hills where we lived, the threat of tuberculosis roamed. "TB" silently slipped into scores of families and robbed them of precious health.

On that August morning when I was 11, the two men were county health officials who had come to take my father to a TB sanitarium. This was a hospital established to treat tuberculosis and isolate infected patients to keep the disease from spreading. My father's shoulders slumped as he slowly walked to the car. I couldn't believe what I was seeing. My father was a wonderful Christian gentleman. A graduate of Simpson Bible Institute, he was a lay pastor who filled the pulpit of several churches. Often he went into jails and held church services. He visited the sick. He read his Bible faithfully, prayed daily, and paid his tithe out of gratitude to God.

Yet this godly man had been diagnosed with TB. Although the scar tissue from his asthma looked like TB, all the other tests for the disease turned up negative. My dad was sure he did not have TB. And he was right. The terrible tragedy was that inside the sanitarium he caught the disease. The more immediate pain was the hurt I felt the morning he left our home. I can still see him being led to the car and the car going away. The only thing I saw that morning was my dad leaving. What I didn't see was how much my life would be impacted by other people's decisions.

Six years later, I was 17 and a senior in high school. Our baseball team had just returned from an out-of-town game. I had played well and felt good. After the bus dropped us off at the gym, I stopped by my girlfriend's home. Ten minutes later the phone rang. It was my pastor. He asked me if I would come home right away. I knew something was wrong. My legs were shaking so badly I could hardly drive. I remember pulling the car into the garage, coming in the back door, and seeing my pastor's face. Then I heard the news: my father had died.

His abdomen had been hurting, and the doctor had diagnosed him as having an ulcer. He was operated on, and after they opened him up they found he did not have an ulcer, but his liver was inflamed, most likely from all the medication he had received for asthma and tuberculosis. He died from the shock of surgery.

In the next few moments, thoughts of my dad's life rolled through me like a wide, powerful river. My father's health, our family's circumstances, and my future were forever altered by the decisions someone else had made.

Since that time, I've seen others' decisions impact my life and those of friends. I grieved with a good friend, devastated when his wife abandoned him. I watched a father left broken when his daughter ran away from home. I knew a man made destitute when his partner stole money from their company. Each of these people know someone else's decision can leave a crater-sized wound in another's heart.

It doesn't matter how good you are, how hard you try, or how much you know. You will face times of pain and loss because of other people's decisions. And though you can't control others' choices, you can decide how you will respond.

2. The lessons of life's circumstances. Victor Frankel was a Jewish Austrian psychologist imprisoned by the Nazis during World War II. In *Man's Search for Meaning*, he tells of being stripped and marching in front of a soldier who looked at each prisoner and motioned to either the left or right with his finger. If he motioned left, the prisoner entered a gas chamber. If he motioned right it was to a slave labor camp.

In the midst of his enemy's cruelty, hunger, and hopelessness, Frankel could have told himself, "Life is not worth living." He could have given up.

Frankel, however, did something different. He found a new reason for living. He used his concentration camp experience to illustrate the age-old advice "When life gives you lemons, make lemonade." Instead of looking down in defeat, he looked outward and learned from others. He began to study his fellow prisoners' reactions to the decisions of their Nazi hosts, decisions he certainly could not control. Frankel concluded that a human being's ultimate freedom rested in the ability to control not his or her own circumstances but his or her responses to those circumstances.

Frankel said as long as prisoners maintained an attitude of hope, they could survive any human indignity. When they abandoned their hope for the future, they would surely die.

In other words, bad things happen to everyone, but hope is an individual choice. Victor Frankel didn't discover this truth—he merely interpreted a vital bit of timeless wisdom for our age. He actually borrowed from a biblical truth spoken by Jesus. In the Sermon on the Mount, Jesus said His Heavenly Father "causes his sun to rise on the evil and the good, and sends rain on the righteous and the unrighteous" (Matt. 5:45, NIV).

Many of life's circumstances are beyond your control. Circumstances can cause you to blame yourself for a "failed decision." Such self-blame is destructive. Victor Frankel didn't wind up in a concentration camp because of *his* decisions. A "failed decision" may not be *your* failure or *your* decision. Sometimes it's really an opportunity to make your decision to keep living with newfound meaning and purpose.

One day I was driving on the freeway when a pillar of concrete fell off of a dump truck I was following. It hit the pavement in front of my car at the same time my car hit it. At 55 miles per hour, hitting an object that size is quite a jolting experience. For the next year I took regular therapy and chiropractic treatment for an injured back and neck.

I did nothing to cause the accident. It just happened. Instead of a black-and-blue memory, the accident has become a watershed moment of personal growth. Though unfortunate circumstances impacted me, they didn't control me. A slab of concrete could ruin my car and injure my body, but it couldn't crumble my hope. Circumstances may have forced me to pull over to the shoulder, but they couldn't keep me from getting back on the road and experiencing life's new journeys.

Circumstances can affect your decisions. In certain cases, they may cause you to view yourself as a temporary failure. They can defeat you or change you—for the good or for the worse. Like other people's decisions, unforeseen circumstances force you to answer the question "How will I respond to people and things that are out of my control?"

3. **The impact of ill-advised decisions.** One of my first jobs was working for a silver mining company in northern Idaho. The idea of owning precious metals got in my blood. Every week I heard new stories of people who had made fortunes in silver mining. Even after I left the company, I still wanted to own silver. At the time, in the 1960s, I was convinced its price would rise. So I started buying silver as an investment. My hunches were right! Over the next 18 months, silver increased

from $1.29 to $2.50 per ounce. I was convinced the market price would go higher, so I kept buying more silver. Even when the price went down, I bought. For the next 10 years the price fell—yet I accumulated more silver.

By the end of the 1970s silver stood at $1.80 per ounce, and my patience had run out. I decided to sell all my silver for 30 percent less than I had purchased it. The timing of my decision could not have been worse. By 1979 the price of silver skyrocketed from $1.80 to $50.00 per ounce.

Where did I go wrong? I had made a sound investment decision to buy silver. I had done my homework. I knew silver would have to increase in value, because its industrial use was increasing while the supply was running out. Therefore, it seemed reasonable that the price of silver would rise. I just got impatient.

My timing to buy was excellent. My timing to sell was poor. My first decision was brilliant. My other decision created the problem! I guess you could say I was an investment genius—as long as I wasn't worried about how much money I had in the end!

This wasn't the first time I demonstrated my exemplary monetary expertise. Many times over the years, on the advice of others or my own judgment, I've sold when I should have bought and bought when I should have sold. Sometimes, for one reason or another, the best-researched and executed decisions just don't work out. Sometimes, like me, you simply need to live with failed decisions that are of your own making. And if you're wise, you won't just wonder, "Where did I go wrong?" You'll ask, "What can I learn from this experience?"

One thing I've learned is that failed decisions are usually inspired by wrong motives. As a young man, I was caught up in many get-rich-quick investments. I had not yet learned that wild speculation is a fast way to lose money, not make it. Over the years I learned that steady, plodding investments usually get you much farther in the long run. Patience and consistency are much better investment tools.

When our decisions go belly-up, we don't like to face the

fact that we failed. Instead, we want to find a reason, an excuse for why things didn't work out right. Human nature always looks for an "out" that relieves us of responsibility. If we can't find that way out, we look for ways to cover our tracks. In most cases this gets us into more trouble than we were in before.

One day King David looked out from his rooftop and saw the beautiful Bathsheba bathing nearby. He liked what he saw and committed adultery with her. As a result, Bathsheba became pregnant. David had to face a failed decision. He needed a way to "prove" the baby belonged to Bathsheba and her husband, Uriah. He brought Bathsheba's husband home from war so the two could spend time together—and so the child would be considered Uriah's.

When Uriah refused to enjoy being with his wife while his war buddies were toughing it out back on the battlefields, David sank to a new level of scheming and sent Uriah back into battle on the front lines, where he would certainly be killed —and he was. One failed decision had led to another. All of David's decisions, rooted in his first decision to be with Bathsheba, failed miserably. Why? Though he convinced himself that his choices were right, each decision was ill-advised, based on self-serving desires.

David eventually faced the truth. He admitted to himself and to God that he was wrong. He admitted that it was too late to undo the wrong he had done. Despite his failed decision, he didn't stop with the question "Where did I go wrong?" He chose to learn from his failed predicament. By admitting his errors to God, by seeking forgiveness and turning from his mistakes, David discovered he could learn from even his worst decisions.

Rather than resign himself to weighty self-judgment, David leaned on God's resources. He discovered true forgiveness and a new start in life by turning away from what he knew was wrong and then choosing to go in a new direction toward God. It is important to note, however, that David faced consequences of his selfish, sinful decisions.

Admitting failure, like David did, may cause you to want to give up. Beware of the urge to stop making decisions. One of my favorite speakers, Cavett Roberts, says, "If a cat sits on a hot stove, it will never sit on a hot stove again. But then it won't sit on a cold stove either. It just gets out of the business of sitting on stoves." Living means daily choosing which "stoves" to sit on—deciding which opportunities to back away from and which to pursue.

Five New Decisions to Help You Endure Hard Times

Sooner or later, we all experience decisions that fail. When you wind up in the wasteland of unfulfilled dreams, when trouble surrounds you, it's time to take a decidedly new approach.

1. Decide to be patient. Anything good in life is worth waiting for. Many times what looks like a great disaster is in reality a temporary setback—if you have the patience to persevere.

Edgar Martinez is a model of patience. Born in New York City, he was one year old when his parents divorced. He went to live with his grandparents, Manuela and Mario Salgods, in Puerto Rico. There he began playing Little League baseball. During his first year he didn't get a single hit! In his last at-bat opportunity of the season, he hit the ball hard but grounded out to the shortstop. At that moment Edgar knew he could be a hitter if he kept trying.

With patience, Edgar learned to hit the ball. He patiently practiced the skills to become a better player and waited for the opportunity to play in the major leagues. In 1992, while playing third base for the Seattle Mariners, Edgar Martinez hit .343, the highest average of any major league player. The boy who struggled through his first season without a base hit became the best in baseball. Edgar Martinez did not accept the results of an *apparently* "failed decision" to play baseball as a young boy. Instead, he decided to be patient. And look where ability, hard work, and patience took him.

2. Decide to rethink your strategy. When your decisions fail, you may need to rethink your strategy. Your "old" way of thinking, acting, or living could be out of step. When your current strategy isn't working, it's worth finding out why and then doing something about it.

In 1965 24-year-old Bob Funk went to work for an employment service. As a placement consultant, he had to find qualified, able workers to succeed at specific jobs. Bob's natural interest in people and his helpful personality were a perfect fit for his new job. Soon he became a branch manager, then division manager. Eventually, he rose to become vice president of the company's Southern and Midwest offices.

The company and Bob grew and prospered through the 1970s. The firm branched into executive recruiting, and, to a small degree, the temporary employment field. Then, in the early 1980s, the company's owner became ill and died. Over the next months, inexperienced managers made many poor decisions, and the company went broke. All of Bob's plans, hopes, and dreams unraveled before him. The words "failed decision" were a stark reality to his bruised self-confidence; his once-proud organization was in shambles.

However, Bob refused to accept failure. He decided to rethink his strategy. He believed the future of the employment industry rested with the small but emerging field of temporary placement. Bob matched his convictions with action. With a few talented associates, he started a new company called Express Personnel Services. The new management team combined their experience, hard work, vision, patience, and the hard but valuable lessons of past failures. They built one of the most successful temporary employment companies in the world.

Bob's new "retooled" strategy paid great dividends. In its first 10 years, Express Personnel Services was ranked three times in the Inc. 500 listings of the United States' fastest growing companies. By 2000 Express was still growing, with over 450 offices throughout the United States and several other countries.

What a difference a failed decision can make! When the bottom fell out of the former business, Bob knew it was time to develop a new strategy. Today that decision has brought him and his colleagues greater success than they could have imagined.

3. Decide to reprioritize. Part of Bob's new strategy was determining what things were more important than others, then putting energy and resources behind those new priorities. Sometimes decisions fail because priorities are in the wrong place. How do misplaced priorities lead to unsatisfactory results?

I knew the owner of a retail jewelry store. He spent a great deal of time shopping for interesting and salable pieces of jewelry. He became a certified gemologist. He was also a terrific salesman. Whenever a person walked into his business, he or she usually walked out with a beautiful ring, pendant, or fine stone.

But the shop's success began and ended with the owner. His employees were not very skilled. When the owner left on a buying trip or vacation, sales plummeted.

When he saw the relationship between unskilled employees and sagging profits, he decided to reprioritize his time and efforts. He took a course on how to hire employees with the skills and attitude best suited for selling jewelry. He read books and articles on how to manage people. Then he put his learning to work. Result: the new employees loved their work. They remained with the business and produced more sales than ever before.

4. Decide to renew your commitment. Sometimes decisions fail because the person doesn't put enough "umph" into his or her decision. Motivational speaker Charlie "Tremendous" Jones says, "Most people are too concerned with making right decisions when they should be trying to make their decisions right. Your decisions become good ones only when you put enough commitment into your actions to make sure the decisions turn out right."

Let's imagine I decide to grow beans in my backyard this summer. I buy a package of bean seeds. If you're committed to growing beans, you'll need a shovel, rake, and a hoe, as well as fertilizer and soil conditioner. It will take time and effort to prepare the soil, plant the seeds, weed the garden, and harvest the crops. This is time and effort I would rather spend reading a good book or visiting friends. The only way I can even hope to see a bountiful crop is if I make a total commitment to do all the necessary steps I've just listed. From my first thought of wanting to grow beans to the time I actually pick them, wash them, cook them, and eat them, I must continually renew my commitment.

Over the years, I've seen folks buy a business without ever getting totally committed to making it successful. Perhaps they don't like to "plant" and "nurture" the initial idea in the "soil" of a sound business plan. They come up with reasons for not "watering" and "weeding" the business by failing to give constant attention to creating, refining, and selling their product or service. Their lack of total commitment makes it look as though they've made a wrong decision. If they renewed their initial commitment in practical, measurable steps, they would see the fruit of their labor. Renewing your commitment can help you see a "failed decision" for what it really is—as an incomplete decision that deserves your full and continued vision, energy, and resources not just from the start, but every step of the way.

5. Decide to rebuild. John Newton was a slave trader. In 1748 his ship was crossing the Atlantic when a gigantic storm engulfed the vessel. Inside the ship lay hundreds of dead and dying slaves bound for the new world. Up on the ship's bridge, Captain John Newton carried on, as uncouth as any man who ever lived.

As the waves pounded his ship into submission, and lightning and thunder rattled his drunken frame, John Newton saw himself as he really was—a man about to die without hope. In the spray and swirl he cried out in terror, "God, save me!"

True to His mercy, God did. The storm raged but did not kill. The ship survived, and so did the man. In His compassion, God lifted a vile slave trader from the depths of his selfish existence and made him a new person.

John Newton looked at the ashes of his wasted, broken

life and decided to rebuild. Out of his wrecked existence he embarked on a life of service to others. He became a minister and spent the rest of his life pointing others to a better way of living, of loving God.

Newton found a language for his new love—music. He began to write songs. Out of his dark past, he found light and a reason to sing:

> *Amazing grace! how sweet the sound*
> *That saved a wretch like me!*
> *I once was lost, but now am found;*
> *Was blind, but now I see.*

Whenever you hear or sing "Amazing Grace," you're experiencing some of John Newton's life and the truth he believed: that God can help anyone whose decisions have failed rebuild. God can forgive you, transform you, and help you rebuild your life if you seek guidance from Him.

What will you do when your decisions fail? Ask John Newton. Ask Bob Funk. Ask Edgar Martinez. Ask anyone who's come up short in life and had to decide how to live differently. Their stories of self-searching and regrouping are models for life, for the new beginnings you can know even in the midst of failure.

TAKING THE FIRST STEP

Never give up! Hope always exists. When your decisions fall apart, never give up. You can find peace during life's storms and comfort in your darkest hours. Let the God who made you lift you to higher ground.

When has a failed decision brought a positive opportunity for your personal growth?

_____

_____

_____

_____

Is there a situation in your life right now that could be the result of a failed decision? Do you need to exercise patience, rethink your strategy, or change your priorities? What would a decision to rebuild look like?

_____

_____

_____

_____

8 Who's in Charge of Your Life?

THE SMALL-TOWN CHURCH HELD A SMALL CROWD. For five days, missionaries from different countries told stories about incredible ways they had seen God work in people's lives. Through prayers that only God could answer. Through physical, emotional and spiritual healings that only God could perform. Through changed lives in individuals, families, and entire communities only God could bring about.

Jim Spencer was a 27-year-old computer analyst who had come to church on a part-time basis for several years. Sometimes he read his Bible. Sometimes he prayed, but not often. He had come to a couple of the evening meetings out of obligation to a friend who told him, "You'll see a whole different side of Christianity that you never knew existed."

Jim felt both curious and skeptical. By the time the final missionary speaker was closing, Jim had a hard time corralling his thoughts to pay much attention to the speaker.

What does missions have to do with me? There's no way I'd ever leave my job and go to another country. I can't imagine working without a regular salary. Besides, all my friends are here.

The rush of thoughts slowed, and Jim heard the speaker: "If God should call you to the mission field, would you be willing to go?" Jim couldn't say "Yes," but he couldn't say "No" either.

"If God is calling you," the speaker continued, "please come forward while we sing, and we will pray a prayer of dedication with you."

The tiny congregation began to sing:

Have Thine own way Lord! Have Thine own way!
Thou art the Potter; I am the clay.
Mold me and make me after Thy will,
While I am waiting, yielded and still.

Jim was not alone in his indecision. His best friend, Bradford, was standing next to him. Bradford knew he wasn't going to be a missionary. He was going to be an engineer after college. Sarah, a third friend in the trio, wouldn't give any ground either. But she couldn't ignore the fact that her heart was pounding faster than normal. She didn't know what she wanted to do with her life, but she was sure it wouldn't be serving in the mission field.

"Not me, Lord."

Over and over she repeated these words. As she continued repeating these words, she realized she was walking down the aisle to the front of the sanctuary. Half way to the altar, the word "No" had faded from her voice. In its place was the answer "Yes." Unwillingness had given way to an inner longing she couldn't explain. She could only say, "Yes—me, Lord."

At that moment, Sarah decided who was in charge of her life. Her two friends Bradford and Jim had decided the same thing as they watched her accept an invitation she would never forget.

You may or may not have ever attended a missions conference. Whether the church is part of your past, or you have no religious ties, the most important choice you'll ever make is whom you'll serve in life. Many people don't consciously choose whom to serve—they just make a number of small, seemingly unrelated choices. When it comes to decisions involving relationships, work, ethics, and responsibilities, they try to "do the right thing." Eventually, without any conscious planning, these choices become habits that create their lifestyles.

Do you approach life this way? Have you ever considered that each of your decisions is tied to a set of values, beliefs, principles, and ideas you consider important? Many people don't stop to think about how their decisions match this core value system. "Why do I believe the way I do? Why is this right?" They never realize the lack of meaning and direction they feel inside could be related to their own values and the unanswered questions "Whom will I serve?" or "Who's in charge of my life?"

Take a few minutes to answer these questions, and you'll accomplish what most people never consider, and that's taking a personal inventory of who or what really runs your life.

Are You Serving Yourself?

"You can't please everyone, so you have to please yourself." These words could be the theme for many people who make themselves the focus of life. Pop religions and New Age thinking are built around this self-serving principle. Countless books and motivational classes promote the conviction of living for self as the best goal in life. Imagine constantly thinking about yourself first, with no one to "get in the way" from your choice of what you want to wear, what you want to eat, where you want to vacation, or what stereo system you want to buy. No wonder serving, pampering, and protecting self is a popular choice!

Is serving yourself a worthy goal for your life? When you make yourself the ultimate authority in your life, you alone bear the responsibility for the results of your decisions. If you observe people who have spent their lives serving themselves, watch them in their final stages of life, and you'll have a pretty good picture of where a life of serving one's self leads a person.

JoAnn's theme song in life was, "I want what I want when I want it." Her parents catered to her every desire. When JoAnn got married, she expected her husband to treat her the same way. He tried to make her happy. But it was never enough. When he didn't make the choices she preferred, she pouted or grew angry. She tried to control his behavior with her emotions. When he let her have her own way, JoAnn was pleasant. However, her selfish desires always exceeded his capability to deliver and please.

JoAnn didn't realize how her behavior affected her husband or her children. Often she manipulated her children's affection. At times she would indulge them, then flip-flop her attitude and emotionally punish them for not meeting her needs. Her inconsistency contributed to their emotional insecurities and resentment. When they grew up, they moved far away from their mother and seldom came to see her.

JoAnn's selfishness produced few lasting friendships. This caused her to grow increasingly isolated. She spent her final years in a nursing home where she made the staff miserable with her selfish demands. Few people came to her funeral.

Think about your own life. Think about how you've spent the past week, the past month, the past several years, and ask, "Am I serving myself?"

Are You Serving Your Senses?

Some people serve their sensual nature. Pleasure comes in many forms, and pleasure is a very demanding master. After you've had a taste of a mouth-watering steak or favorite dessert, it's hard not to want more. The same is true for those who've found temporary pleasure in a relationship that's merely physical: usually once is not enough. They want more.

Servants of the senses must continually devote an increasing amount of time, energy, and resources to feeding their appetites. The senses promise fulfillment but produce an ever greater hunger.

Stephen fell into this trap. His appetite for sexual pleasure grew beyond his ability or willingness to say "No." His promiscuity led to two broken marriages and countless damaged relationships. His acquaintances laughed at him. His children no longer respected him. His lack of integrity crippled his business career. Eventually his sensual appetite drained him of his time, his emotions, his finances, and his enjoyment of life.

What about you? How important are sensual pleasures, including food, music, activities, entertainment, and sex? As you think about how much time and energy they consume, ask, "Am I serving my senses?"

Are You Serving Money?

Because money is a driving force in our culture, it's very easy to make money our goal. Whether we earn it, hoard it, or spend it, money is somewhere in our thinking. If someone asked, "How much money is enough?" I think a lot of people would answer, "Just a little bit more than what I have."

That was Mary's response. A successful legal secretary, she

dressed well, drove a nice car, and lived in a comfortable townhouse. Her husband, Bill, was a tradesman, and on paper their combined income covered all of their basic needs, including health care, savings, and a modest amount for weekly entertainment. Yet they were in constant financial trouble. Their favorite lament was "There's always too much month left at the end of the money."

Mary thought about money constantly as she thought about all the bills they needed to pay. Yet she rarely thought twice about the new clothes, kitchen items, and compact discs she regularly bought. She grew angry that her employer didn't pay her more. She didn't like the fact that a lack of money was causing her to make "so many frustrating decisions in so many areas of my life." How big a role do you think money played in Mary's life?

How big a role does money play in your life?

Are You Serving an Institution?

Some people give their lives to an institution. It may be a company, a volunteer organization, or a longtime local club. An institution can take the form of a school, a church, a business, or a government. People who are loyal to an institution usually consider themselves as working for "a higher, greater good." They sacrifice personal needs and wants for the larger community. The institution's success becomes their success. What happens, however, when the institution fails to live up to their expectations?

Institutions will disappoint you. You may serve an organization for years without any assurance that the institution or the people in it will show appreciation.

Is there an institution to which you feel loyal? When you consider all that you've given and your expectations for return, ask, "Is my life about serving an institution?"

Are You Serving Others?

Occasionally a rare individual comes along with the nobility of spirit and the discipline of character to live a life of service to others. The major motivation of these worthy individuals is to give to their fellow human beings. While their goal is not to gain fame or wealth, occasionally their efforts are rewarded.

In 1928, an eighteen-year-old Yugoslavian girl named Agneus Gonxha Bajaxhire decided to give her life to serving others. She joined a religious order that sent her to India. In 1950 she formed a religious order called the Missionaries of Charity. Although the work started in Calcutta, the order now operates hospitals, schools, and orphanages, and gives shelter to lepers and the poor and dying in cities around the world. While her goal has been to serve others, the founder became one of the best-known people in the world. We knew her as Mother Teresa, the Saint of the Gutters.

While you and I may never smell the stench of an open sewer or touch the withered limbs of a dying man, we can consider what it means to serve the needs of others.

When you think about where you spend your free time, your thoughts, and your money, what faces come to mind? Then ask, "Is my life about serving others?"

Have You Considered Serving God?

People who consciously decide to serve God with their lives can be found in almost any area of life. Their calling and work isn't limited to the pulpit or a foreign mission field. Their motivation stems from their decision to give God all they are and all they hope to become. While they may be *committed* to the institution of the church, the needs of others, and the necessity of meeting their basic needs of money, shelter, and health, they *choose* to serve God.

You'll find many advantages in letting the God who made you direct your life. God knows everything about you. He knows your strengths, your weaknesses, your motivations, and your desires. Most of all, He knows what's best for you. We often have such limited vision and make limited decisions. But God sees the big picture. He knows what's best in the long run. If you let God make the final decision, it will be the best decision.

God has an eternal agenda. While He cares about the details of your life, He keeps it all in perspective with His hope and plan for you to spend an eternity with Him. Your eternal home is more important to God than your earthly home. He helps you make decisions that will prepare you for a positive and enjoyable existence in this life, but most important, for a glorious future.

When you put God in control of your life and let Him be your final authority, He will give you internal and eternal peace. Then you will have confidence about your decisions. If you know you're doing God's will in life, you don't have to spend a lot of time second-guessing yourself. You can focus on what needs to be done. We have His Word on it: "You will keep him in perfect peace, Whose mind is stayed on You, Because he trusts in You" (Isa. 26:3). "Trust in the LORD with all your heart, And lean not on your own understanding; In all your ways acknowledge Him, And He shall direct your paths" (Prov. 3:5-6).

If you agree that it makes sense to turn your life over to an all-powerful, all-loving, all-forgiving God, who is more capable of running your life than you, take action. In business, action may take the form of a memo, a voice mail message, a fax memo, or an E-mail message. When it means coming to God freely, just as you are, action means prayer. If these words express what you feel and believe, they are no longer just words but a sincere prayer that will put God in charge of your life.

Dear God,
I know You're in control of all things.
I know You're more capable of running my life than I am.
I give to You, now, control of my future.
I give to You, now, my decisions.
My dreams, goals, and aspirations I place in Your hands.
Please make my life what You want it to be.
I'll follow, to the best of my ability, where You want me to go.
I'll do, to the best of my ability, what You want me to do.
I'll seek, to the best of my ability, to be the kind of person You
*   want me to be.*
I give myself to You.
In Jesus' name I pray. Amen.

OBEDIENCE: THE KEY TO A MEANINGFUL, FULFILLING LIFE

Several years ago I gave several speeches about prosperity. One day a dentist named Don Wilson asked if he could buy me lunch. I have a policy of saying "Yes" to this kind of invitation! Dr. Wilson said he had heard about my talks and wanted to know what I could tell him about prosperity. I replied that most of my research was done from reading the Bible. I suggested he read all the passages in the Bible that contained the word "prosperity" and that after he had read them we could have lunch again and discuss the subject.

A few weeks later we got together for lunch. Dr. Wilson had read the references, and I asked him what he had learned. He said, "Prosperity is the result of obedience." He was right. The Bible promises to bless people who are obedient to God's will.

The greatest challenge for anyone who wants to serve God is to learn God's will for his or her life—and then do it. We may not know all that God wants us to do; however, we can know and practice His principles found in His Word—the Bible. Though it sounds incredibly simple, anything God tells us to do in the Bible is part of His will for our lives. When in the Ten Commandments we read, "Thou shalt not bear false witness" (Exod. 20:16, KJV), we know it means you should not lie about other people. If I say something about someone else that I know is untrue, I'm not doing God's will for my life.

Jesus said,

Why do you call Me "Lord, Lord," and do not do the things which I say?

Whoever comes to Me, and hears My sayings and does them, I will show you whom he is like:

He is like a man building a house, who dug deep and laid the foundation on the rock. And when the flood arose, the stream beat vehemently against that house, and could not shake it, for it was founded on the rock.

But he who heard and did nothing is like a man who built a house on the earth without a foundation, against which the stream beat vehemently; and immediately it fell. And the ruin of that house was great (Luke 6:46-49).

Jesus was telling us that people who build their lives on principles that conform to the Bible will withstand the storms of life's worst trials. Those who build on false principles will see their labors destroyed.

Mark Twain once said, "It's not the parts of the Bible I don't understand that bother me—it's the part I *do* understand." He expressed a truth I'm sure we've all felt at one time. The more we know about how God wants us to live, the harder it seems to be totally obedient. Yet, as difficult as it may be, obedience is the secret to growing and maturing in God. You cannot violate God's instruction for your life and then expect God to lead and guide you.

If you choose to give God your life, obeying His principles is not an option. Obedience is the key to your growth and development. As you do what you know God wants you to do, He shows you more of His plan for your life. When you let God be in charge of your life, your purpose, your service, and, yes, your decisions, He'll guide you and help you grow into the person He planned you to be.

TAKE ACTION! WRITING YOUR PERSONAL MISSION STATEMENT

Look at the annual report of any successful company, and you'll see its mission statement. This is a brief declaration of why the company exists and whom they serve. Imagine running a multimillion-dollar company without a mission statement, without any clear direction or stated purpose of who you are and what you're trying to accomplish. If you wouldn't run a business that way, why would you live your life without a stated mission and purpose? Do you believe your life is worth more than the most successful companies on the planet? Consider what God has paid for your life. If you said yes, it's time you wrote your own personal mission statement.

TAKING THE FIRST STEP

Today I decide to answer the question "Who's in charge of my life?" by writing my own personal mission statement:

The purpose of my life is to _____

_____

_____

_____

_____

The words I would like to have on my tombstone are these:
Here lies_____, who spent his
[her] life _____

_____

_____

    If someone did not know me and followed me around for
a month, would he or she conclude that I'm motivated to accomplish what I wrote above?   Yes _____ No _____
    Based on my actions and words, what would he or she
say is my life purpose?

_____

_____

    What changes do I need to make to create a greater har-
mony between my stated life purpose and my actions?

_____

_____

    Make a decision today to turn your life over to God. Let
Him be the ultimate authority of your life. Take time each
week to review your personal mission statement. As you learn
more about God through the Bible, prayer, and serving Him,
look for ways to apply the lessons to your daily decisions.

CONCLUSION
DECIDING TO LIVE DIFFERENTLY STARTS TODAY

The sky was foreboding and dark. Clouds swirled in a nervous wind. Nature seemed to cry out in agony as three men hung from wooden poles. Their indignity and suffering lay bare before the crowd who had gathered to watch the sport and drama of a public execution.

The Man on the middle pole looked at soldiers near His feet, who were gambling for His only possessions: His clothing. Next to them, cheering and jeering in anger, He saw the people who clamored for His death. He glanced at the horizon and saw 10,000 angels prepared to come to His rescue. At the sound of His voice, they could liberate Him from this unseemly human spectacle. The choice was His: He could end His public humiliation and physical suffering, or remain on the pole and fulfill the promise He made to His Father. He looked at the crowd and said, "Father, forgive them, they do not know what they do" (Luke 23:34).

With those words His decision was made.

One of the men next to him cursed and said, "If You are the Christ, save Yourself and us" (Luke 23:39). This man had made his decision too. He felt the Man on the middle pole was a fraud. And so he continued to die, a convicted thief, dying the way he had lived—negative and bitter to the end.

The man on the other pole had a similar background. Like his sarcastic counterpart, he had made a lifetime of poor decisions. Like his fellow thief, he was breathing his last minutes of life. However, unlike the other man, he was convinced the Man on the middle pole was no ordinary human being. He had watched Him endure the pains of execution, and he sensed He was innocent. He cried to the thief who had cursed

Him, "Do you not even fear God, seeing you are under the same condemnation? And we indeed justly, for we receive the due reward of our deeds; but this Man has done nothing wrong" (Luke 23:40-41).

Then, to the man on the middle pole, he said, "Lord, remember me when You come into Your kingdom." Jesus replied to him, "Assuredly, I tell you, today you will be with Me in Paradise" (Luke 23:42-43).

The two thieves represent two distinctly different destinies. They represent the ends of life's spectrum for you and me. The first thief chose to deny the One who offered unconditional love, acceptance, forgiveness, and eternal life for all who believe and follow Him. For the first thief, dying was the sad end to a sad life. The second thief saw the Man on the middle pole for what He was and is today, the Son of God who came to take on the selfishness, greed, arrogance, hatred, and every other imperfect expression of human nature that weighs you and me down every day—and will eventually result in our physical deaths.

The Man on the middle pole—the God who became a man, the visible Christ who made the invisible God someone we could see with our own eyes—decided to voluntarily suffer the death you and I deserve because of our sin. He was totally innocent, yet He went to the Roman "electric chair" and received the death sentence every human should receive.

With which thief do you most closely identify? Like both men, you may be suffering and scarred from bad decisions. If so, I want you to know one thing: *It's never too late to make a change in life.*

Perhaps it's time to be dissatisfied, impatient, less tolerant, and even angry at where bad decisions have brought you—unsettled enough to make needed changes. Today, at this moment, you can begin a new way of living, a new way of deciding about how you will lead your life, strengthen your marriage, nurture your friendships, build your business, and direct your energy, time, and resources to what really matters most in your life.

Everyone wants to experience greater freedom, abundance, meaning, direction, and purpose. How you achieve these things is the adventure and journey of your life. The "how" of getting there is different for each person. Regardless of how you make the journey, I believe the eight critical questions and decisions in this book are wrapped up in one ultimate question, and your subsequent decision. Both thieves considered it, and so must you and I: **Will you turn your ultimate destiny over to the One who is ready to forgive you for every bad decision you have made?**

Will you allow this One to guide you in every decision, large or small? Will you allow this God to direct you to opportunities, places, and people in a way no current media personality, counselor, or popular spiritual guru could ever do? Will you let Him take you, just where you are and as you are, and lead you to a destiny better than you can imagine?

You can answer that question by writing your response to one of these two questions:

1. I would like to hold onto my life like the first thief and continue to make all of my decisions on my own without the help, guidance, and direction of the all-powerful, all knowing, all-loving, all-forgiving God, because _____

_____

_____.

2. I would like to give the control of my life to God, like the second thief, and make all my future decisions by calling on the help, guidance, and direction of the all-powerful, all-knowing all-loving, all-forgiving God, because _____

_____

_____.

Take a few minutes and think about your written response. How will you implement this decision? _____

_____

_____

Now go to the last page of each chapter and reread the First Step, the practical thing you can do today to make each of these eight critical decisions an agent for change in your life. Use the following section as a personal journal to track your progress in these areas over the next three weeks. In the space below, write what resulted from that First Step within the three-week period. A practical outcome is a changed attitude or action you can measure and describe. Example:

As a first step toward deciding whom I will call my friend, I've made my own list of seven characteristics to look for (and to practice myself) in a friendship. These characteristics are . . .

Now it's *your* turn!

Chapter 1: Who Will You Call "Friend"?

As a practical first step toward deciding who I'll call my friend, I will _____

_____

_____

Chapter 2: Where Will You Live?

As a practical first step toward deciding where I'll live, I will _____

_____

_____

Chapter Three: What Will You Do for a Living?

As a practical first step toward deciding what I'll do for a living, I will _____

_____

_____

Chapter 4: How Will You Handle Money?

As a practical first step toward deciding how I'll handle money, I will _____

_____

_____

Chapter 5: How Will You Deal with Temptation?

As a practical first step toward deciding how I'll deal with temptation, I will _____

_____

_____

Chapter 6: How Will You Respond to Adversity?

As a practical first step toward deciding how I'll respond to adversity, I will _____

_____

_____

Chapter 7: What Will You Do When Your Decisions Fail?

As a practical first step toward deciding what I'll do if my decisions fail, I will _____

_____

_____

Chapter 8: Who's in Charge of Your Life?

As a practical first step toward deciding who is in charge of my life, I will _____

_____

_____

Let's return to the execution scene. If you identified with the first thief, after having looked honestly at the results of your decisions, is there anything there that might cause you to identify with his counterpart, the second thief? If you identified with the second thief, again looking at the results of your decisions, what caused you to decide that? What have you learned about the power, faithfulness, and love of God?

Your responses to these questions mark the end of this book and the beginning of new choices you will make from this point on. Your life and your future can be as exciting and rewarding as you want them to be. It all starts with what you do with the 8 Critical Lifetime Decisions—beginning *today*!

Because Your Decisions Do Make a Difference

A Personal Invitation

I have no doubt that the decisions you make as a result of this book will bring some tremendous, positive changes in your life. I believe this because the 8 Critical Lifetime Decisions are based on timeless, proven principles that work. I would like to know how they work for you. I would like to hear the stories of how your life is fuller from acting on these eight very important decisions.

Simply type or hand-write your story and mail it to me:
Ralph Palmen
The Palmen Institute
9833 Crystal Lake Drive
Woodinville, WA 98072
You may also fax your story to me at 425-489-9409 or E-mail it to rponlakedr@aol.com

Be sure to include your full name, address, and appropriate phone number, fax number, and E-mail address when you write. Please also look at my web-site for more information and assistance: **www.Ralphpalmen.com**.

I look forward to hearing from you. Thank you.